LAITY, CHURCH AND WORLD

LAITY, CHURCH AND WORLD

Three Addresses

by

YVES CONGAR

of the Order of Preachers

Translated by

DONALD ATTWATER

93230

Bt
1920
.C74

HELICON PRESS
BALTIMORE, MARYLAND

Nihil obstat Adrianus van Vliet, S.T.D. *Censor Deputatus*

Imprimatur E. Morrogh Bernard *Vic. Gen.*

Westmonasterii, die 6a Aprilis, 1960

The *Nihil obstat* and *Imprimatur* are a declaration that a book or pamphlet is considered to be free from doctrinal or moral error. It is not implied that those who have granted the *Nihil obstat* and *Imprimatur* agree with the contents, opinions or statements expressed.

LAITY, CHURCH AND WORLD was originally published in France, under the title SI VOUS ÊTES MES TÉMOINS, by Les Editions du Cerf, in 1959.

Library of Congress Catalog Card Number 60–16436

Made and printed in Great Britain

The first of these addresses was given during the Fourth Franco-German Week at Freiburg-in-Breisgau in 1958, the subject of the conference being Spirit and Freedom. The second paper was read before the *Religiöse Bildungsarbeit der katholischen Gemeinde Stuttgart* in 1958; and the third before a gathering of clergy and Catholic Action lay leaders of the diocese of Rottenburg, who were studying the problems of evangelization today.

Owing to common ground in the subject-matter, there are a few small repetitions, but each has its own shade of relevance. The spoken form of the addresses has been retained throughout. The last two were originally delivered in German.

CONTENTS

HOLY SPIRIT AND SPIRIT OF FREEDOM

I have to set before you what the fact of Pentecost means in relation to the theme of Spirit and Freedom. I want to do this in as practical and concrete a fashion as possible; and therefore in a way that touches human life as it is lived. For you are men. What sort of men? Christians, of course, and as such you are citizens of the City that is above, fellow citizens with the blessed in Heaven. But you are also men engaged in the life of this world, in this year of grace; and accordingly you seek to live your Easter and your Pentecost, on your own behalf and on behalf of your fellows, in the world of men, on this human earth, here and now. Therefore it is not enough for me to talk about what the Holy Spirit brings to Christian life *in the Church*; I must also show what that Spirit means to Christian life *in the world* as it actually is. And I will begin with that: man, as a child of Easter and Pentecost, in the world of the twentieth century. Afterwards I will speak of man, as a child of Easter and Pentecost, in the Church of the twentieth century—which, of course, is also the Church of all time.

1

IN THE WORLD

Threats to personal freedom

In the first place I must briefly examine man's situation in the world of today from the point of view of our being called to be men of spirit and to be free, and in as much as Christianity concerns this vocation.

There are two outstanding characteristics of the world in which we live that go in opposite directions, and at the same time offset one another: one is the importance given to the individual person and his freedom; the other is the quest for power through organization, with its huge undertakings and a gradual socialization of life.*

There is a tendency in modern society to attach an over-riding value to individual freedom. In France especially, freedom is thought of as a right of complete self-government for the individual, the possibility for each person to do what he likes, a freedom limited only by the equal similar freedom of others and by the general will.† But, on the other hand, contemporary individuals are at the mercy of two gigantic powers, the

*This far-reaching twofold movement has of course often been remarked on; it has a place, for instance, in Pierre Teilhard de Chardin's great cosmic-Christian epic, *The Phenomenon of Man* (London, 1959).

†Cf. art. 4 of the Declaration of the Rights of Man and the Citizen (1789): "Freedom consists in being able to do whatever is not harmful to someone else; each man's exercise of natural rights has no limits except those that ensure enjoyment of the same rights to other members of society." In a purely external, individualistic democracy wherein the right of lesser communities is more or less disregarded (as in France), there is real danger of the "general will" becoming an oppression of minorities by the majority, and turning into state totalitarianism.

nation-state and big industrial enterprise. Material well-being, a good standard of living, has become dependent on large-scale industry, which is more and more based on the use of machinery. Inevitably, this has produced four results that condition our lives; they are these:

(1) Cut-throat competition, which makes life a nerve-racking business at every level. People today are far too keyed up: they are for ever trying to go quicker, to overtake a rival, to pass an exam or get a job that will make them better off—"better" meaning "ahead of others".

(2) The pouring out of an endless stream of propaganda and aggressive publicity that aims at winning over a huge public, whether in favour of some manufactured product or a set of ideas or a political programme. I need not say more about this; everybody knows it, and it has often been analysed and denounced: the devices and resources of propaganda are used to force human judgement, till eventually people are unable to think and decide for themselves.*

(3) Educational institutions with powerful resources, large factories, industrial cities and other agglomerations: such concentrations of people of their nature encourage a mass psychology.

(4) And then the intervention of public authority, "the state", responsible for the common good of its people. This intervention takes the form of "planning"; it seeks to harmonize the powerful forces on which human well-being depends in a rational, scientific way. Forecasting of future

*Charlie Chaplin's films *Modern Times* and *A King in New York* were to the point.

conditions and control of factors in them are based on statistics. And so life becomes increasingly socialized.

It is obvious that a common tendency of these four factors is towards reducing human beings to the state of a mere mass of creatures. This has been written about a good deal, particularly by the historian of civilization J. Huizinga.* It is his opinion that this "collectivization" of life takes away from man decisions that he ought to make for himself; it dehumanizes him and leaves him a prey to mob characteristics, to cruelty, intolerance, sentimentality, formlessness: in short, to the opposite of what should characterize a human person and a truly humanistic spirit.

It is true that the individual person has reacted against all this, and that the reaction is strong and widespread: but what form does it take, in what direction is it going? Man is in danger of being as it were torn in two, so that the life-blood would be drained away from his inner self and spiritual freedom. There is the risk of letting his life be split into separate compartments: one is his working life, the hard struggle for material existence, planning, all the socialized activities which reduce him to being an item in the general mass; the other is his leisure time, a counterbalance which he uses to try and tone up his nerves. As soon as he can, he gets away from towns and factories and offices, away to hills and fields and beaches, by car, by bicycle, on foot. Once there, he flings away all the constraint he can (symbolized by the throwing off of clothing). He stops thinking about anything. He has escaped.

*See, in English, his "Conditions for a Recovery of Civilization" in the *Fortnightly Review* for 1940, pp. 394 ff.

But has he not also escaped from himself?* What good is it doing him as a man? Freedom for the body, yes; but what about the deeper freedom of the soul, the freedom of a being who is responsible for himself? The danger in this flight from work by wandering, in swopping blouses for bikinis, is that it leaves no room for the human person itself; it is forgotten that there are other needs to be satisfied, such as the things of the mind, spiritual freedom, development of one's own character. Is the *whole* man being taken seriously when attention is given only to his job and to keeping up with the Joneses, and to making up for the resulting weariness of spirit by simple diversions and "getting away from it all"?

Some compensations

It must not be forgotten, however, that contemporary life itself includes certain not inconsiderable humanizing resources. In spite of everything, in spite of "stateism" and planning and bureaucracy, natural communities have not entirely disappeared: first and foremost there is the family, that great well-spring and sheltering ark of human healthfulness. In those communities man learns his need to protect himself and to associate with others in a more humane way than is provided by benefit-societies or associations arising out of his work. And modern techniques, so far from destroying the

* "You are going fast—but where to? You fools don't trouble to think about that. . . . What are you running away from? Alas! you are running away from yourselves. . . . We understand absolutely nothing about contemporary civilization if we do not recognize straight away that it is a world-wide plot against every kind of inner life. Alas! Yet freedom is simply within yourselves, you idiots!" (Georges Bernanos, *La France contre les robots*, pp. 137–138.)

5

worth of certain recreations, spread them abroad and increase their possibilities. I am struck, for instance, by the renewed and big part taken in people's leisure by books, drama, music and singing—these have poetical values, and so spiritual ones. Or again, hiking and camping can contribute to a quest for things of the spirit. And, furthermore, the techniques of the machine, by multiplying ways and means, not only offer new and considerable possibilities of personal culture but strongly encourage their use.

The first stage of the industrial revolution has lasted two hundred years and has now, I hope, touched rock-bottom. It brought into existence a new world of slaves serving machines, and that has resulted in the emergence of a huge body of "hand-to-mouth wage-earners", a proletariat, a mass of depersonalized individuals without any cultural background. When we find that in some countries nowadays, notably France, the better educated classes have more religious faith and practice it better than the workers as a whole, we are looking at something besides the reflection of economic conditions. Educated people have a personal culture which enables them to attain faith more easily, because they are already acquainted with things of the spirit. This is still the state of affairs for a minority of privileged persons; but it is permissible to think that it will extend to very many more people in the years that lie immediately ahead.

Statistics suggest that this is not a sheer flight of imagination. If the machine sets men free from the necessity of certain toil, automation will do this still more. But there is still the question an Indian is said to have put to an American who boasted of a new machine that would save ten minutes: "And what will you do with the ten minutes?" The existence of this sort of fallacy does not alter the fact that technology by itself is powerful to civilize and humanize. What Ruskin said is still true, that everything can be made in factories, except men. Nevertheless technology does open a way to an increase of culture. But it is not simply that it reduces human toil: for its own extension and perfecting it requires more better-educated men. In the world today it is *a fact* that, when men leave the natural conditions of primary activities (e.g. agriculture, fishing, forestry), they go less into the secondary activities of industry or building and construction than into the tertiary activities of office work, study, services, schoolmastering, the learned and commercial professions.* What is happening is what is bound to happen—an ever-increasing extension of what is, on the whole, that middle-class life which is the ambition of everybody everywhere.

So I do not want to ignore the opportunities for "humanization" to be found in our technological world as I have briefly analysed it. But these possibilities are obviously far from denoting a direct and effective increase of the life of the spirit. And indeed the object of this paper is to point out what Easter and Pentecost can do for contemporary man, not only as a remedy for his ills but as a positive principle of life and health.

*Colin Clark's terminology is generally accepted. See J. Fourastié, *La Civilisation de* 1960 (Paris, 1947), p. 25. Figures given for U.S.A.:

	Primary activities	Secondary	Tertiary
1830	72·8%	12%	15·2%
1940	19·3%	31·1%	49·6%
Forecast for 1960	16·4%	26·5%	57·1%

Man's great need

There are more difficulties in the way of the life of
the spirit for man today than for his predecessor in
medieval Christendom; and yet he has more need of it.
I can hear somebody say: "What? You want to talk
about life of the spirit to people harassed like us, who are
embroiled in the competition and demands of the world
we live in?" And I reply, "Yes. And to them more than
any, because they have a very urgent need of it." It is
a case where the useless is the most useful, the irrelevant
supremely relevant.

A man must have a point deep down in himself in
which he can be himself, where he finds and lives his
own life. He must as it were inhabit himself. And it is
at this inner point that he must find freedom, shaking
off and rising above the shackles that constrict his life,
including the tyranny of his pleasures (for they can
enslave him); but at the same time he keeps his contact
with the world of men, for the condition of human life
consists, as Maurice Merleau-Ponty has put it, in
"being unto the world through a body."

No doubt it could be *proved* by a process of reasoning
that only the divine communication which we call the
Spirit of God is able to bring this about. But I prefer
simply to *assert* that it is so: not on my own "say so",
but *as a fact* that is attested by the clearest and most
unexceptionable testimony that you can ask for, that
of the men and women we call saints. Granted that it is
only saints who experience this in the highest degree;
but every Christian, every person who is indwelt by
God's Spirit, has, or can have, this experience in a lesser
way. What this experience is I would express in two
sentences reminiscent of, but more philosophical than,
Luther's *The Liberty of a Christian Man*: Through the

8

Holy Spirit, the man of Easter and Pentecost is himself, but he is not isolated in himself; he can free himself from the compulsions of his world, while remaining committed to his engagement in its affairs.

The theme of Spirit and Freedom is concerned with man's return to himself, with a refusal of that alienation that would reduce him to being an element in history or in industrial production, free only to compensate for this by "escapes" that reinvigorate the human animal without giving new life to the human person. The man who prays, who knows that God calls him, who is conscious of the divine presence and those divine "touches" that are always accompanied by some demand on us, that man has a personal existence. "The man who prays is never a nobody," said Ernest Hello. Romano Guardini has properly emphasized what may be called the anthropological value, the value for a man simply as a man, of recollectedness and—what is obvious enough—of adoring worship.

The same is true of Sunday, in addition to its absolute value as the Lord's Day. It is the day on which a man stands upright. All the week he has, so to speak, been stooping over the ground, at his lathe or his engine or his desk, at her cooking-stove and the children's mending, doing the work of the world. But on this day he is reminded that he is called to be a citizen of the City that is above; he remembers that he has a soul, and that this makes him a king, above all those things at which he toils like a slave. It has been well said that "The purpose of the Sabbath is to make a breach between man and his functions, to prevent the identification of man with his functions,"* and *in this*

*C. Tresmontant, *Essai sur la pensée hébraïque* (Paris, 1953), p. 164. It is a Jewish saying that "On the Sabbath day the

9

connexion the same can be said of the Christian Sunday. On this day the Church says to us, completing her message of Ash Wednesday: "Remember, man, that you are spirit and that you will return to the Spirit".

On the one hand, man is subjected to the grinding tyrannies of mass-production and to the indignities of rabbit-warren housing, public transport at the rush-hours, and the rest of it. On the other, he seeks a purely external freedom in inadequate recreations and physical "escapes." But if he has an inner life, if he is an "inward" man, he finds a real self beyond these warring elements. Faced with enslavement to propaganda and advertising, he makes within himself a corner of resistance to the wolves of conformity and mob enthusiasm. The vast increase through technology of means which may be used for the oppression of man by man, for the destruction of man by man (Yes, this includes atomic weapons) call imperatively for conscientious protests on the same scale. It is absolutely necessary that men should find, in an inner life and the deepest convictions of conscience, means to save their own manhood and that of others.

Faith always makes persons. A religious faith prevents, for example, a worker from being wholly and and only a paid "hand", dedicated solely to his work and to the proletarian cause; but this is not so much because such a faith may lead to "bourgeois" or conventional ideas with regard to established authority. Christianity does not prevent him from being a worker or from being active on behalf of workers' interests. But it does make *impossible* that process of reduction, which

poorest Jew is a king, his wife a queen, his children royal princes".

10

Marxism exacts and brings about, from man to worker or a means to production, and from worker to proletarian, fully mobilized for service in its class war. Accordingly, though they are not on the same level with it, faith and a religious life are opposed to Marxism: not only doctrinally, in their positive teaching, but in their attitude towards man and what sort of a creature he is. In the same way, though it is not *of* this world, the Christian religion is a power *in* the world. There is an outstanding opportunity for Christians in this age, one of whose greater problems, greater every day, is to harmonize planning with the individual's nature and rights, the social organization of life with the building up and development of persons. But to cope with that, Christians have got to go back to their first principles.

We have got to be very careful, too, that in acquiring depth and an inner self through religion and spiritual life, we do not cut ourselves off from the world. It cannot be denied that there are dangers here: it is a common reproach to us Christians that we selfishly withdraw into a cosy shelter provided by "spiritual" absorption in the needs of our dear little souls. However liberated we may be from the restrictions imposed by a mechanized world, we are still "in the world", with a part to play in its life and history. As Christians, what we need is not *less* spirituality, but more and more of it, and above all a biblical, that is a genuinely Christian, spirituality.

Theories of freedom: the Christian answer

It seems to me that the principal theories of freedom that influence people today can be reduced to three:*

*I exclude Sartre's existentialism, which few people know about or are interested in.

the idea of it that derives from Rousseau and the Jacobins (particularly influential in France), the Marxist idea and the Stoic idea.

The first of these looks on freedom as an absolute good, and one to which each individual is entitled: it is only a matter of bringing about the external conditions which encourage its development, and—since it is an absolute good—its greatest possible development. For Marxists, the notion of freedom is simply formal, and ineffectual enough. For them, true freedom is a state that has to be attained through liberation from the "alienations" and hindrances that afflict mankind. It arises from a social situation in which man has been emancipated from oppressive conditions, is conscious that a social plan has been realized in fact, and sees himself as collectively making his own history; he understands everything now and so will never again be put upon by anything or anybody, for his life will be made up only of things that he will do, and will be conscious that he does, collectively.

So, for democracies of the Western type, freedom is something individually owned, and the individual must simply be allowed to use it. For the People's Republics, it is hoped for as a benefit that is collective as much as personal: the consequence of man's full control of his destiny and of a perfect harmony between man and his labours.

With all their differences, the Rousseauist and Marxist ideas have this in common, that they see freedom as a state of emancipation from constraints that are *outside man himself* and his mind. Making the classical distinction between "freedom *from*" and "freedom *to*", we should say that in this conception of it freedom is essentially a freedom *from*, a right rather than a duty, a liberation from something external to man. Here freedom is not looked on as an inward and positive quality of existence, which is what it is for Christianity. In a way it was for Stoicism too, for Stoicism promoted the notion of freedom as inner independence of whatever can make a man morally a slave. It had its eye particularly on the emotions and disturbances that are provoked in the mind by outside events and nature's contrary ways. The remedy offered was to seek this inner freedom—a personal perfection—through ridding our will of its passions and bringing it into line with the cosmic order of the world, the kind of "general will" diffused in nature. It was a high ideal; and Christianity has sometimes been represented as resembling Stoicism, but in fact it is profoundly different.

Like Stoicism, but to a far greater degree, Christianity refuses to reduce freedom to a matter of free will, the ability to do this or that, the freedom of unconcernedness, or to a liberation from external constraint. Rather is it a spiritual quality of human existence, a perfection or characteristic of man in himself; and, as it actually exists in this or that person, there can be different degrees of it. St Augustine and St Bernard speak of a "freedom from coercion and restraint", freedom to be oneself, to live one's own life; but beyond that of a "freedom from wretchedness", that is, from evil, error and sin, which are more inside ourselves than outside us.

Freedom, then, is not simply freedom from whatever prevents me from ploughing my own furrow in my own way without interference: it is, positively, a matter of our ability to share in goodness and truth. It is, indeed, always a question of man's return to himself, but here man has a pattern that is both above and within himself: to return to self is to return to the image of God.

To be rid of some external compulsion is only one degree of freedom, and not the highest. The truth is that man could never be more free than were he, by some blessed impossibility, to reach the state of being unable to sin—like God and, in the created order, Christ. (We are a long way from Gide, at the opposite pole in fact.)

The highest degree of freedom is not to govern oneself, but to be wholly governed by God: not forgetting that, while God is outside and above us, he also dwells within us. Because he is God, he is in some sense within us physically; spiritually and morally he is within us through the free gift of his Holy Spirit "in our hearts" (Gal. 4:6). Thus it is *from within*, gently, that he moves us towards what is good, to the true good. The pressure or attraction under whose influence we act is the Holy Spirit himself. Here the whole subject of Christian freedom is involved; and that would entail discussion of the whole "programme" of Christian life and the Christian ethic as a *paschal*, an Easter programme, concerned with the achievement of spiritual freedom. "A price was paid to redeem you; do not enslave yourselves!" (1 Cor. 7:23; cf. 6:20, 7:22, Gal. 5:1).

The essential and distinguishing thing in the Christian teaching about freedom, differentiating it from Stoicism, is that it takes account, not of two factors, but of three. Not simply man and those circumstances external to man that eventually enslave and tyrannize over him; but man, external circumstances, God. And it is God that makes all the difference. Stoicism tried to find freedom through ridding our will of its passions (*apatheia*) and bringing it into line with the general will of nature, the world's cosmic order. The Christian's cosmos is quite different: it is not a world of cosmic

14

nature, but a world of God's designing, of the free saving design that the living God follows therein.

Accordingly, Christian freedom consists in the perfect agreement, not of an "apathetic" will with nature, but of a love-intoxicated will with the saving will of God as it is shown forth in Jesus Christ. "Philip, whoever has seen me, has seen the Father. . . . I am the way" (John 14:9, 6).

True religion is not isolating

Now this will of God, in action, as we see it in Jesus our way, is love and service, the humble service of love; it is love coming into this world to take its evil on itself and to overcome it in the manner of the Suffering Servant (cf. Isaias 52:13–53:12 etc.): it is what St Paul calls "the wisdom of the Cross".

In those meaningful symbolic images that the thirteenth century was so fond of, Free Will was some-times represented climbing a ladder, and the ladder was Christ's cross. Adam thought, Sartre thinks, we all think in our unregenerate moods, that the way of freedom is the way of self-will. It is not. It is the way of dependence, of lowliness, of giving oneself to others. Freedom is made real only in love: not in being "for myself", wrapped up in self, but in being "for others" and "going out" to them. . . . If it be taken in its properly Christian meaning, surely it is right to say that the life of the spirit, so far from isolating us, ensures that we live "in the world"—and that we do so freely.

But who dare believe so firmly in that as to act accordingly? Who dare stake his all, his whole life, on the Gospel's "He that shall lose his life for me shall find it"? Who dare lose himself in Jesus Christ, believing that so he will find himself again? Who dare give himself in the certainty that thus he will possess himself, and rise above himself for love's sake with the assurance that thus will he be free?

The Holy Spirit and the Church

The Spirit of Pentecost created the Church, or rather, gave life and impetus to it; he launched it into the world as something in the world but not of it, having a mission to the world, with an existence and a life of its own, given from on high: made up of men, and yet a divine institution.

It is a little like the work of natural creation as it is presented in the book of Genesis: God first makes a being of a certain kind, and then gives it life; or like Ezechiel's vision of the valley of dry bones: God brings together the scattered bones to make skeletons, he clothes them with sinews and flesh, and then he breathes life into them. So it was with the Church. First it was given form. That was the work of Jesus Christ during his public ministry: he chose and sent out the twelve apostles, he revealed the Father and announced the good news of the Kingdom, he instituted the sacraments thanks to which we were to share in his mystery through the contacts of our senses. So the essential lines of the Church were laid, the building was in place, the body ready. There only remained to give it breath and life: that was the work of the Holy Spirit.

So we see that the making of the Church involved two "moments" or stages. This is a fundamental point for our subject, and it is important to get a proper grasp

16

of it. I will first explain it from the standpoint of principles, showing the Holy Spirit's relation to Christ; and then from the standpoint of activity, what that Spirit does in the Church.

Christ is one divine person, the Holy Spirit is another, a person in himself;* but he is the Spirit *of Christ*, the Spirit *of the Son*.† Thus the Holy Spirit has a "mission", a "coming", of his own: just as the Father sent the Son into this world and the Son came in Jesus Christ, so the Father sends the Holy Spirit to dwell in those who follow Christ. But the work of the Holy Spirit's mission is not *his* work, something independent and self-contained: it is the work *of Christ*, who has already done the Father's work, given the Father's message. . . . The Spirit consecrates and sanctifies *Christ's* apostles; he gives them understanding of what *Christ* taught them ("The truth-giving Spirit . . . will not utter a message of his own. . . . He will recall to your minds everything I have said to you": John 16:13, 14:26); he makes men holy through *Christ's* sacraments.

If we now look at the Holy Spirit's work and activities we notice two points that take us to the heart of this second part of our subject. The first point is that: *The Holy Spirit is sent into men's hearts; he makes Christianity intimate and personal.*

With the help of the Bible we can (as the early Fathers did) apportion the various parts of God's work among the divine persons of the Blessed Trinity; and

---

*John 14:16–17: "I will ask the Father, and he will give you another to befriend you", or "give you another Paraclete."
†Spirit of Christ: Rom. 8:9; 1 Peter 1:11. Spirit of the Lord: Acts 5:9, 8:39 2 Cor. 3:17–18. Spirit of Jesus: Acts 16:7; Rom. 8:9–11; Phil. 1:19. Spirit of the Son: Gal. 4:6. In John 20:22 the spirit that Jesus breathes on his disciples is the pentecostal Spirit; cf. 1 John 5:6 ff.

we then see what can be called, in human terms, an ever-deepening and closer concern of God with his creatures.

There is first of all the Creation, the making of the world and of all things, visible and invisible: this we can attribute to the Father, who overrules all. "I believe in one God, the almighty Father, maker of heaven and earth", says the *Credo*, which is built up on the threefold pattern of the Trinity. Then there is the Redemption, the work of the Son. This too is, in a way, an external work. The Son is sent *into the world*, and he there establishes a means of salvation as an objective fountain of grace. At the prayer and in the name of the Son, the Father sends the Holy Spirit in order that this life may be made ours.

We are told that the Son was sent into the world, but that the Holy Spirit is sent "into our hearts".* His particular part is to bring to the heart of each one of us the work that Christ did objectively for all. The Holy Spirit, the third and last of the divine persons of the Trinity, is the bond, in God, of that inter-flow of life that constitutes the fellowship of the Three in oneness; and it is for him to apply Christ's work to each of us, to bring personally to the heart of each and every Christian Christ's grace, Christ's love, Christ's mind, Christ's power.

The second point is that: *The Holy Spirit is given to the Church; we receive him only in the fellowship of the whole.*

While the Holy Spirit makes Christianity inward and personal, he is given to the whole Church, as Church, to be its unifying principle. He is in each member,

*Cf. Gal. 4:4–6 and Fr Congar's *Mystery of the Church* (London, 1960), pp. 24 and 52–54 (quotation from H. B. Swete). And cf. pp. 23–25.

intimately with each, but he is one and the same in all. J. A. Möhler pointed out that the Spirit was given to the disciples just when they were all together and of one mind in prayer and love.* Jesus had already said that "Where two or three are gathered together in my name, I am there in the midst of them" (Matt. 18:20).

The Spirit then is given to each, but in company with the rest. He is the principle of unity, as the soul is for the different parts of the human organism. He dwells within each person, in his heart or spirit, as the inner law of fellowship and unity. My soul is not given to my hand apart from my head or my heart. If my members are separated one from another, they cease to live. Just so He who is the principle of personal faith and individual Christian life is given us within a unified organism and for a unifying purpose. The office of the Holy Spirit is precisely to bring together in unity the gifts that he implants in individual persons.

After all, we already know that, from the Christian point of view, a person fulfils himself and attains freedom by "going out" and giving himself to others, in a spirit of humble ministering love. Every time St Paul speaks of the charisms, the spiritual gifts, with which the inner life of Christians is so richly endowed, he emphasizes their variousness, but shows that they are given through the members of the Body for the use and benefit of all (1 Cor. 12; Rom. 12; Eph. 4). The Spirit is indeed the living principle of personal religion; but he is given to each man or woman as a member of an organic whole and according to the part each has to take or the contribution that he or she has to make to the unique life of that Body. In this way Christianity

*Cf. two relevant passages in Möhler, quoted in Congar, *op. cit.*, pp. 54–57.

brings together two things that are often in opposition to one another: "inwardness" or personal life, and the communal principle or unity.

Suppose it is a question of the public and institutional aspect of the Church. Then, if you are one of the lay faithful, you have been given the Spirit that you may believe; if you are a bishop, you have been given the Spirit that you may be a shepherd, to care for and direct the flock that the Holy Spirit has entrusted to you (Acts 20:28). Or is it a question of the hidden life of the soul? One person has the grace of prayer, and uses it for the good of others; a second person has the grace of strength or of giving testimony or of comforting: hiddenly, through the working of the Holy Spirit, these are all brought together to do Christ's work in that communion of saints in which we declare our belief in the *Credo*.

I have already quoted Merleau-Ponty to the effect that man has to "be unto the world through a body". Could not the situation of the Christian be characterized as "belonging to God through, by means of and in the organic unity of a Church"?—the Church that is People of God and Body of Christ. . . .

We can now understand why, where Christian life is concerned, the man of Easter and Pentecost is faced both by an unquestionable duality and by the necessity of unity.

We cannot deny a certain duality or push it out of sight; we often meet it, expressed in different words and from different points of view: communalism and mysticism, static and dynamic, closed and open, letter and spirit, institution and event, legality and spiritual gifts, official and personal, priestly and prophetical, and who knows what else. There is a duality because there are two missions, that of Christ and that of the Holy

Spirit; but we know these two missions are for one and the same work. To deny one or other of the two terms is not the answer; the answer is to hold fast to both in their unity and to make their harmony with one another real to ourselves, for that is the nature of God's work.

The religion of Pentecost is *at the same time* the religion of inward Spirit and of Church, of direct "contact" and of mediation. Not to recognize that, to see only a purely inward, personal and direct relationship of religious people with God, is to fail to recognize the true religious relation as God has revealed it and shown it forth in and through Jesus Christ. And, on the other hand, to pass over the element of personal inwardness, and stress and pay attention to the institutional side alone, is to ignore an authentic aspect of God's work and of the Christian reality.

What this means for the laity

There is no doubt whatever—and it has been remarked on more than once lately—that not enough has been heard about this personal aspect of religion; or at any rate that it has been too much confined to the personal life of prayer and union with God. Too little is said about its various significances in the Church's life: Christian freedom, its part in the maintaining and development of doctrine, initiative in the Church, the whole business of the laity's "coming of age" (I should not much like that expression "coming of age" had not Pope Pius XII himself used it, at any rate for the field of apostleship).*

Like all omissions of the kind, the frequent ignoring of such matters sometimes provokes people to seek compensation in irresponsible fault-finding, a sort of

* In his address to the men of Italian Catholic Action on 12 October 1952.

flirtation with freedom, which is rather unhealthy. Are we going to leave the privilege of meeting these aspirations to Christian bodies that are not Catholic, and so cause much harm to the truth of an authentic religious relationship?

The important truth that emerges from what has been said above, and which must guide us in what remains to be said, is this: Lay people are not only *objects** in the Church, objects though they are of her goodness and care; they are also religious *subjects*,* and therefore active persons. They are not only *made by* the Church, in as much as she is an hierarchical institution; they *make* the Church, in as much as she is *congregatio fidelium*, the society of the faithful, as the Church was defined in the middle ages. That the laity are personal subordinate subjects is true; it is also true that they must conform themselves to the Church's unity, a unity that has its own structure, rules and requirements. But this unity is not that of a merely external association (such as a club): it is the unity of a body living in all its parts, of a fellowship, a communion of persons.

In short, a Christian is not simply a bit of the material on which the Church works, any more than a man is simply a bit of the material of history or of industrial production or of governmental power. Every person exists in himself, he has a destiny of his own, that he cannot relinquish to anybody else. But it must be observed, in passing, that this does not work out in exactly the same way in civil society and in the Church. The proper and specific object of the Church is the

---

**Object* in the sense of a person (or thing) to whom something is done or about whom somebody or something acts or operates (passive), as opposed to the *subject* that thus acts or operates (active). [*Trans.*]

supernatural destiny of persons; but this is not the case with civil society.

Lay people, then, are persons in the Church. With truly Roman precision and conciseness, canon law declares: "By baptism a man becomes a person in Christ's Church, with every Christian right and duty" (Canon 87). Being a juridical document it understands "person" in a juridical sense, as the subject of rights and duties; and that is useful for our purpose. The Church says that the Christian has the rights and duties of a person: among them, the rights and duties of freedom are certainly not the least. These are our concern; so let us look at them from two points of view, that of inner freedom, a deep personal quality, and that of external freedom.

For lay people the essential point is the duty, and the corresponding right, to become *adult Christians, free men*. These two terms are practically equivalent. A free man is one who governs his own actions, who does not submit to other pressure than that of his own choice. *"Liber est causa sui,"* says St Thomas Aquinas, following Aristotle: the free man is the self-determined man. But the adult—I am of course referring to moral and spiritual adulthood, a state to which the grown-up in years does not always attain—the adult is a man who no longer has to be warned, encouraged, supervised in order that he may act. When we were children we went to Mass because we were told to. Plenty of grown men and women go simply because they fear "what the neighbours might say" or because of the reproofs that will fall on them if they do not. The spiritual adult goes because he knows what he is about and has personal spiritual convictions within himself that move him to go. And so he goes freely.

23

To be a Christian with an adult faith is a very big commitment. On the negative side, for example, it involves putting away attitudes and behaviour that are childish, mechanical, legalistic, governed more or less by *tabus* and apprehensions that are more reminiscent of the religions of heathenism than of faith in the living God, the God, "who is, and ever was, and is still to come" (Apoc. 1:4; Exod. 3:14). And here I believe is the crux of the whole matter—faith in the living God. This is not the place to set out the reasons; but I am convinced, after much thought about it, that the real key to an adult Christianity is to be found in living faith—not some "religious attitude" or other—and in faith in the living God—not in some celestial Leader, Eternal Axiom, Great Architect or Supreme Being.

The need for adult Christians

I have two more deep-seated convictions in this matter. One is that the age we are living in has a special need for such Christians. Father E. Mersch has written nicely that "some animals need a shell because they have not got a skeleton". If this be true, we may well think that Catholics need to be given a strong spiritual skeleton, when we look around and see on all hands that the old sociological frameworks of Catholicism are being called in question, shaken loose and damaged by modern conditions and events.

A Christendom that is going to renew itself and live in the present cannot, apart from rare survivals, start from a basis of regulations, social set-ups, the favour of public authority, social pressure, as was the case in the past. It has to start from personal conviction, from the witness and glowing influence of Christians who are such from their very depths. The time has gone by

nearly everywhere when civil powers would pay attention to priestly authority expressed in terms of that
authority. But Christian witness, arising from the convictions of a conscience dedicated to the living God, is as
strong as ever: yes, even against the powers of the
world, as we saw, for instance, in Germany when the
Protestants of the "Confessing Church" stood out
against Hitler in the name of their faith in Christ, who
alone is Lord. For that we need really adult Christians,
free men who have been set free by Truth (John 8:32).

But I am also convinced that this to a great extent
depends on the clergy. Only an adult priesthood can
increase the number of adult lay people. There can be
no witness from the laity unless the priesthood comes
up to the ideal (to the best of its ability—the finest of us
are but poor creatures!) that was expressed recently
by the rector of a seminary and quoted with approval
by the Archbishop of Chambéry: "I do not want to
turn my students into clerics who have the spirit of
Levites, but into priests who have the spirit of prophets."

As things are, do not ecclesiastics often seem more
ready to give orders than to educate, to insist than to
uplift? In my book on laity I have quoted several
statements from Catholics on this score;* here I want
to quote a critic from outside, whose words are nevertheless worth pondering. This is what Amiel wrote in
his *Journal*: "Catholic thought cannot conceive per-
sonality as conscious and master of itself. Its daring and
its weakness come from the same cause: lack of responsibility, subjection of conscience, which knows only
slavery or an anarchy that proclaims the law but does
not obey it because it is outside itself. . . . 'Right-wing'
Catholicism never gives its followers freedom: they have

Lay People in the Church (London, 1960), e.g. p. 46.

to accept, believe and obey, because they never grow up." There is more than one ambiguity in that passage; it is a caricature, and false accordingly: but it is worth thinking about for all that.

It can hardly be denied that, in taking a side or expressing an opinion, Catholics often try to shelter behind some authority, some law or decision or extract from an encyclical letter or papal address: in other words, they try to find a shell. Is it because they have no skeleton, no backbone, no nerves, no muscles? When I saw a fine film about Maxim Gorky's younger days I was struck by a sentence that occurred in it twice: "Be careful never to shelter your conscience behind somebody else's conscience."* If you want to hear the verdict of an orthodox Catholic, and a cardinal at that, read Newman's answer to Gladstone about papal infallibility; he explains how the pope's authority, so far from annulling the individual conscience, presupposes the strength and faithfulness of that conscience, and he ends humourously: "Certainly, if I am obliged to bring religion into after-dinner toasts (which indeed does not seem quite the thing), I shall drink—to the Pope, if you please—still to Conscience first and to the Pope afterwards."† That is to say, it is the honouring of the first toast that would give meaning and value to the second.

Among the Church's tasks and pastoral undertakings I would give the formation of Christian *men* precedence over organizations and systematic groupings. To be sure,

---

*Cf. what St John Fisher wrote to Thomas Cromwell: "Not that I condemn any other men's conscience. Their conscience may save them, and mine must save me." [*Trans.*]

†*Letter to the Duke of Norfolk* on occasion of Mr. Gladstone's recent Expostulation, 1875 edn., p. 66.

such things are wanted; but we ought never to forget
what our Lord told the Pharisees, that "The sabbath
was made for man, not man for the sabbath": we have
to appreciate the significance of those words for church
matters, as well as their moral truth. In the middle ages
they were fond of expressing the same idea in the words
"The Church is not the walls but the faithful"; and I
would like here to recall a remark of Bernanos: "It is a
fine thing to put social programmes on paper. But it is
important to know what sort of people you have to
carry them out". For the Church, indeed, that is the
main question. In his address of 18 February 1946,
Pope Pius XII declared that the Church's influence
differs from that of political societies through the fact
that "she acts on man in his personal dignity as a free
being, at his very heart; she strives to form men . . .,
and she does her work in the depths of each one".

Everybody knows that it is difficult to make men
free. Often they are the first not to want to be free;
having to make their own decisions is a heavy burden,
and they like other people to do it for them, as Dos-
toyevsky set out so forcefully in "The Legend of the
Grand Inquisitor" in *The Brothers Karamazov*. Yes, it is
difficult to make men free—and it is risky, too. Many
do not know how to use their freedom, and some know
too well how to abuse it. But there are risks naturally
attaching to the use of freedom even short of real
misuse. Freedom calls for open discussion and frank
give-and-take: it is therefore a threat to dogmatism (I
do not say "to dogma"!). Freedom involves the accep-
tance sometimes of uncertainties and hazards; these are
things that alarm a short-sighted authority, or one that
is too self-conscious, an authority that is inclined to
"paternalism". And, even when it works within the

limits that it must not over-step, the spirit of freedom cannot fail to express itself outwardly in certain dissentient attitudes that insist on asking questions.

Freedom in the Church

I have just said "within the limits that it must not over-step". The faithful Christian has to be free *in* the Church, but not *with regard to* the Church, that is to say, not with regard to the essential things of that institution which Jesus Christ founded for our salvation: dogma, sacraments, apostolic authority, unity in the faith. We are free in the truth; it is, indeed, the truth that makes us free (John 8:32); but we are not free with regard to the truth. Please keep this well in mind: it is fundamental to what I am now going to say, which is concerned chiefly with the Christian's external freedom in the Church.

First I want to call your attention to that great field in the Church today, as at every other time, wherein Catholics enjoy extremely wide spiritual freedom. It is something very real and positive; and if some people are hardly conscious of it, it is perhaps because they are not much concerned about the life of the spirit and of charity. Please just think what scope there is for *religious initiative* in the Church. Within the sacred limits of unity in the faith and communion with the successors of the Apostles, you are free, not only to pray how you like, to sing your spiritual song to your own tune, but also to undertake some apostolic work or other: if you want to, you can found a new religious congregation, and give it a striking habit or the quaintest of head-dresses. I am not joking! There is no end to the originality of the saints, whom the Church celebrates individually, each under his or her own name

28

—there are only 365 days in the year, so our calendars can only give us a small sample of them.

Recognition has always been given in the Church to what would be called in English the law of conscience: its traditional name is *lex privata Spiritus Sancti*, the individual or "private" law of the Holy Spirit, as distinguished from *lex canonum*, the external law that applies to everybody. It was recognized that the relations of a man's conscience with God go beyond the bounds of his relationship with the Church's canonical organs. A person has spiritual aspects which are not reducible to terms of ecclesiastical common form.*

At the same time there was and is always in the Church the fundamental principle that I have set before you: the Holy Spirit is the Spirit *of Christ*. He does not come to do some new and different work, but to do that work whose essential elements have been fixed by the Word made flesh. There is no law of the Spirit which can go against these essential things, no "inner voice" that can truthfully gainsay Christ's own work: "No one can be speaking through God's Spirit if he calls Jesus accursed" (1 Cor. 12:3).

Let us glance at the question of freedom of speech and public opinion in the Church. Here the documentation is again very extensive and includes, as well as private writers, the utterances of weighty official authorities. So, in contradiction of what I have just said, I can shelter my conscience behind other people's! But I am sure you will appreciate that the subject is one of special importance and delicacy.

*Abundant references could be given for this subject. An historical article of special English interest is "Grosseteste [bishop of Lincoln] and Papal Sovereignty", by Brian Tierney, in the *Journal of Ecclesiastical History*, vol. vi (1955), pp. 1–17.

I invoke then the authority of Cardinal Stritch, archbishop of Chicago, in his address to the Catholic Press
Association in 1954*; and I quote the synodal statutes
of the archdiocese of Cologne of the same year: "Lay
persons are not forbidden to protest against the short-
comings of members of the clergy, by a brotherly
remonstrance and with a due sense of their own
deficiencies." Then I appeal, not to Caesar, but to a
pope. In addressing the international congress of the
Catholic press in Rome in 1950, Pius XII declared that
public opinion is an attribute of every normal society
made up of people who are conscious of their respon-
sibilities, and that the absence of a free public opinion
would be a disease in social life. He went on briefly to
apply these truths to the Church, "for she is a living
body," he said, "and something would be lacking to her
life were there no public opinion in it, a want for which
the blame would rest on pastors and faithful".

Freedom of speech in the Church is, of course, only
one chapter in the whole business of making religion
personal. In a short space I can only pick and choose my
topics; and it is with full consciousness of being
deplorably "bitty" that I select, to end with, one of the
chief enemies of this personal undertaking and ideal—
juridicism or legalism.

Freedom and legalism

I repeat with emphasis what I have said about the
relation of the Spirit to the foundations, faith and
sacraments and apostolic institution, that were given
by the incarnate Word. And I am not attacking either
law or its enactments—I believe it would take a lot of

*Quoted by R. C. Hartnett, "Public Opinion within the
Church," in *America*, 19 June 1954, pp. 315–317.

torture to make me utter a single word against canon law itself. It is true that the spiritual man is emancipated from the law as law, that is, from an external coercive obligation, because by love he has made it an inward, personal thing. But in as much as God is not yet "all in all" (to use St Paul's unsearchably deep expression), we stand in need of the discipline of an outward law; with St Thomas Aquinas, we must look on it as a wholesome aid to the spiritual self and our efforts to deepen it. From this standpoint, a strictly theological value can be given to Newman's explanation of the considerable increase, in modern times, of doctrinal and disciplinary action by ecclesiastical authority, especially by the central authority. Rationalism, atheism and the anarchy of thought, he said, demanded this strengthening of the Church's teaching and controlling authority; and this power, he added, "viewed in its fulness, is as tremendous as the giant evil which has called for it" (*Apologia pro vita sua*, 1886 edn., pp. 243 ff.).

The Church's law is holy, her authority is holy; but they exist for the benefit of the spiritual life of her children. Once again, the Church is not walls, or barriers either, but people, the faithful. St Thomas teaches that the Christian law consists principally (and his "principally" has very nearly the meaning of "essentially") in the inward grace of the Holy Spirit; secondarily, and as auxiliary to and in the service of the first, in the external things, dogma, sacraments, authority, rules and the rest (*Sum. theol.*, I–II, cviii, a.1).

Juridicism or legalism results from forgetting, at any rate in practice, this relationship of service and subordination: an absolute value is given to what are means to an end, such importance is attached to them that in practice everything seems to revolve round their observance. It is well known that forms, "correctness", tend to acquire an inflated value and to be mistaken for the whole of religion. The Church's history records one reform movement after another: and these reforms sprang up, precisely, in the name of the *meaning* of things, as against undue concern about rubrics or observances; or in the name of the Gospel, as against the temptation to exclusiveness and pharisaism. In our individual lives, but also in the life of the totality of us gathered in the *Ecclesia*, there is need for a perpetual revision of means, in the light of how those means originated and of the ends to which they are directed. At this very time this is happening in a most striking and effective way in the field of public worship.

We must always beware lest *legal* aspects are allowed to capture and monopolize *spiritual* matters. This can in practice lead to regarding orthodoxy as essentially a defence of the clergy's authority, and to exalting obedience as *the* virtue of the good Catholic. The Church is sometimes looked on too much as an external, juridical society, one in which the characteristic relations are those of authority with its subjects, of subordinates with their rulers. Of course this is one aspect of the Church; but she has it *after her own fashion*, and her most characteristic and searching laws are those required by communities of persons, in particular the sort of community that is a *communion* or *fellowship*—a fellowship of life, of salvation, of sanctification and of witness, a fellowship of which the Holy Spirit is the personal indwelling principle.

Such a community of men on this earth needs rules and regulations, an authority, the relations proper to a society. But all that is to minister to and help the spiritual life of persons, and it must not weigh too heavily or be excessive. Laws that are too burdensome are apt to produce rebels or hypocrites or people whose character is infantile. Too many regulations and external obligations, said St Augustine, do not accord with man's condition according to the Gospel, which is that of son, not of slave; St Thomas and the whole of the middle ages echoed Augustine, and the same idea was voiced at the Council of Trent. In all this the Church has constantly to contend against her natural or human element, so that she may be obedient to the Spirit of Christ; that Spirit which, acting in her and in each of her members, bishops, priests and laity, is so profoundly hers.

A problem for everybody

One last remark. What I have been saying might give a superficial hearer or reader the impression that, in the Church, the quest for freedom of spirit is a sort of concealed conflict between those below and the "higher-ups." It is not so. Spiritual freedom is a question of *Christian existence*; the rulers in the Church are in the first place Christians, and they have to face the question as much as do those who are ruled, each at his own level. St Augustine used to say to his flock (using those verbal alliterations of which he was so fond): "Vobis sum episcopus, vobiscum christianus", "I am bishop over you, but I am Christian with you".

I appeal to you to think about what I have said in the light in which I have said it all through from the beginning: the light, that is, of the Holy Spirit, the gift of Easter and of Pentecost, the soul of the Body of Christ; the Spirit that breathes in each member of that Body according to what he or she is, the faithful as

33

being subordinate "in Christ", the rulers as being our leaders "in the Lord". There is no question of a capricious, irresponsible freedom, an unregenerate freedom; each of us shares in the freedom of Christ's Easter and his Pentecost in proportion to our dedication to him, to the degree that we are bound to him. To be God's servant, that is the only Christian freedom.

THE LAITY IN THE CHURCH,
PAST AND PRESENT

My title implies two aspects of the subject: firstly, clear teaching on the place of lay people in the Church and on their part in the Church's mission in and to the world; secondly, an estimate of how this has worked out in history. We have to study and understand the position today in the light of the past, both the recent and the more remote past. There is no question of disparaging the generations that have gone before us—each generation does what it can. But at any given time there are special circumstances and needs, and these can be better understood if attention is also paid to those of other times.

It is clear that the laity are not in the same situation today as they were fifty or sixty years ago. There has been no change in essentials, of course: the Church today is the Church of all time. But the Church *of all time* is the Church of *today* in that she adapts her forms of life and activity to the requirements *of today*. We will illustrate this by considering, one after the other, the spheres of worship, of faith and apostleship, and of influence on secular affairs.

Worship

When I was a child, somebody made me a present of a handsome Mass-book, of the kind fashionable in those days, or a bit earlier. It was finely bound, with gilt edges, and the little islands of text were surrounded by imitation miniatures and sham illuminations. But it was no good for following Mass with; at the beginning of the canon it said: "We will not translate the mysterious words of the canon . . .". I must admit that when, much later on, I had a real missal in my hands I was rather disappointed: I was expecting all sorts of extraordinary things that were not there!

Nowadays it is quite different. Large numbers of people follow Mass with the help of a complete missal. I have seen the change taking place. You know how it is: parents sometimes do not notice how their children are growing because they see them every day; but somebody who sees them only after six months or a year notices the change at once. And so I, having for long had to preach or give addresses in the same places every three years, have from time to time been made aware of the greatly increased use of missals and the big advances in the liturgical life of parishes. We are still far from the ideal; but at least we have begun to realize what is meant by the words *plebs tua sancta*, God's holy people.

The Church's life of faith

Where belief is concerned, things are very much changed from what the Fathers tell us about the end of the fourth century. In those days, anybody and everybody used to discuss abstruse questions about the doctrine of the Holy Trinity; a man could not take his shoes to be mended without the cobbler talking about "substance" and "hypostasis". In a famous article,* Newman made an impressive collection of evidence showing the part played by the laity in safeguarding the true Trinitarian faith throughout the great crises over the Arian heresy; and he remarks elsewhere: "In all times the laity have been the measure of the Catholic spirit; they saved the Irish Church three centuries ago, and they betrayed the Church in England."†

I am a great believer in this preservation of the faith in the hearts of the faithful laity, and in a few years time we shall be celebrating a centenary that is very significant for this matter. About the year 1660, after a long, thorough and ruthless persecution, the Catholic priesthood was destroyed in Japan, and with it every external manifestation of the Church. The first missionary to return was Father Bernard Petitjean, who in 1865 opened a little wooden chapel in Nagasaki. What was his astonishment when Japanese at once came to pray in it, particularly before a statue of our Lady. They were the descendants of the seventeenth-century Christians, who from generation to generation had secretly kept and handed on the faith, and with it the practice of baptism and of prayer and the rules of Christian life. Somewhat similar happenings are recorded elsewhere. And is it not true that beyond the "iron curtain"—which begins only a few hundred miles to the east of us—the same sort of thing is happening every day?

This is a very real aspect of the part that the laity

*"On consulting the Faithful in matters of Doctrine", in *The Rambler*, July 1859, pp. 198–230. Newman's ideas about an effective laity are summarized in L. Bouyer's *Newman* (London, 1958).

†*Lectures on the Present Position of Catholics in England*, 1908 edn., p. 392.

plays; but it must not be exaggerated, nor made into something independent, as if the laity were the only people in the Church. I will try and put it in perspective in a minute. But it is quite certain that, when lay people are kept in tutelage and treated more or less as children, they become as indifferent to the Church's faith as to her life. Let me give you an illustration from history. In the Scandinavian countries the Protestant Reformation was introduced easily and without upheaval. In 1637 a Norwegian-born Catholic priest, calling himself John Martin Rhugius, came secretly to Larvik in Norway. In the country parts he met people who, a hundred years after the Reformation had begun, did not know that any religious change had taken place; they had noticed that their pastors had altered a number of things, but they thought this was in accordance with orders from the pope for "all over the world."*

That was a bitter harvest of the medieval practice of too easily talking about "implicit faith"† where the simpler faithful were concerned; this led to the famous "faith of a charcoal-burner" that the Reformers criticized so severely. It is a sort of religion by proxy, in which somebody else thinks and decides for us. Submissiveness to our bishops is absolutely necessary; but it is obvious that a church made up of Christians who are wholly passive, even from the point of view of belief, will be but a listless, anaemic church. The good health of the Church requires that the faithful be active, even if (as we see in families and schools) robustly healthy children are a bit more difficult to keep in hand than those who are ailing and spiritless.

*See Sigrid Undset, *Saga of Saints* (London, 1934), p. 290.
†"Implicit" in the sense of not expressed, not understood in any measure, not made living and personal. [*Trans.*]

Today especially, what are wanted are conscious Christians, whose faith is alive and personal, penetrating their whole being. If Father Mersch be right when he says that "some animals need a shell because they have not got a skeleton", then surely Catholics need to be given a strong spiritual skeleton, for all around us the old sociological frameworks of Catholicism are being questioned, and weakened by modern conditions and events. If Christendom is to be renewed for its task today, it is no good looking for external supports, government favour and the like, that are no longer there; we have to start from personal conviction, from the witness and influence of men and women who are Christians through and through. In a word, we need people who know and cling to their faith as something living and personal.

Having come so far, I must touch on this question: How is this function of the laity with regard to the faith to be thought of from the standpoint of sound doctrine concerning the Church? The answer—like the answer to a number of other questions—depends on our giving its right sense and meaning to the word "Church". This may surprise you; you may think everybody always does that. I am not so sure. I make it a habit, every time I meet the word "Church" in writings new or old, to ask myself what sense is given to it here, what meaning lies behind it. Try it for yourself; and you will find that perhaps nine times out of every ten the word "Church" in fact signifies the hierarchy of bishops, the governing body, sometimes even simply the pope, with or without the Roman congregations. As if a body consisted only of its controlling organs, or a people of its government ministers and senior civil servants!

No! The Church is a body that is living in all its parts,

wholly vitalized by its soul, and that soul is the Holy
Spirit. The laity too have the Holy Spirit. But the soul
does not animate all parts of a human body in the same
way, because those parts are differently placed and have
differing functions; my soul animates the cells of my skin
that it may live and feel, the cells of my brain that it
may be an organ of thought and control of movement,
and so on. So it is with the Church's members. Spiritual
vitality is given to them all: it is given to some simply
that they may live, grow and show forth Christian life;
to others, that they may lead and guide.

And there is constant give and take between these
and those, in such a way that there is living contact
between the life of the first and the direction given them
by the second. For they, the laity, are not directed from
outside, mechanically, like a stick that is used by a man:
direction comes from the organs of a body of which they
too are members, whose one life they all share, and they
contribute actively to that life, every one in his own
place. Thus, just as my mind "takes in" the sensations
felt in my skin, so the governing organs of the Church
absorb the thoughts and feelings of the whole body of
the faithful—without, of course, becoming merely an
echo of them.

The Church's apostolic life

It follows that lay people in the Church, while being
subordinate to authority, are not and must not be
simply *objects** (though they are the objects of the
clergy's care). Within the unity of the organic spiritual
whole that I have described, they are living, thinking
*subjects.** They are real persons, with initiative and a
life of their own that cannot be given up.

*See the footnote on p. 22.

Obviously their activity is directly governed by the necessity of conforming with the deposit of revealed truth received from the Prophets, from Jesus Christ and from his Apostles; this deposit is a trust of all the members of the Church, but its guardianship belongs to her bishops in an altogether special way. The laity cannot be legitimately active in the sphere of ecclesiastical authority, whether for ruling or teaching, because they have not received the Holy Spirit for that purpose (apart from exceptional cases). Their proper sphere is that of Christian faithfulness.

A very useful study could be made of this idea of Christian faithfulness, what the Gospel calls with such deep insight "keeping the word".* It is not merely a matter of remembering; if it were, a book or a gramophone record would be more useful for the purpose than a soul. But it is precisely to our souls that Christ's "word" is entrusted. It has in the first place to be "kept" by putting it into practice, and finding the motive force of faithfulness in this loving obedience; and not just faithfulness but a living faithfulness, that makes use of what Christ's word tells us in all life's various situations and demands and needs.

By so doing, the faithful not only keep the word, they also contribute to its development. There is, for instance, the influence that the laity have had, right down to our own time, in the development of teaching about our Lady† (in my opinion, exaggerations in this matter are to be blamed more on certain theologians than on the Christian people at large). But I must emphasize a

*See John 8:51 ff., 14:23, 15:20, 17:6; 1 John 2:5; and cf. Luke 2:19, 51, 11:28.

†Cf. Y. M. J. Congar's *Lay People in the Church* (London, 1960), p. 274. This book is referred to hereafter as *Lay People*. . . .

41

4

point of much practical importance. We shall see presently that lay people stand, as it were, on the frontier where Church meets world, and that their *own particular* mission is to bring Christian influence to bear on secular life. The laity's part in doctrinal development in the course of time will evidently be greater, or at least more original, in some fields than in others. For instance, where it is a matter of Christianity giving answers, in accord with Christian understanding, faithfulness and thought, to questions or demands raised by the contemporary world: questions of culture, of art, of apologetics, and so of expressions rather of Catholic atmosphere and outlook. And then in the realm of what is called the Church's social teaching, which is simply a developed expression of certain aspects of Christian teaching about man. Pope Pius XII, for example, recognized this expressly in his message to the Federation of Christian Workers' Movements, meeting at Düsseldorf in 1955.*

Following up what I have said about the true meaning of the word "Church", I want to take a quick look at how, through a radiant faith, lay people in a measure carry on the Church's work as our mother. We must not make the mistake of thinking that this motherhood can be seen only in the ministering of the sacraments or when the Church's ministers instruct or discipline her children. When, in a family or a parish or a Catholic Action group or a students' society or in some other way,

*"Through its researches and pooling of information your federation can help to clarify the picture of this situation [concerning wages and salaries]; and by so doing it will render a service to the Church, whose social teaching not only has continually to direct practice, but is also itself directed by practice. It is the same for all pastoral work that seeks to meet the needs of our day" (quoted in *La Croix*, 27 May 1955).

you help to form a little centre of faith, prayer, love and striving after good, you are to that extent enabling the Church to give birth to Christianly-living souls. And what about good parents in their homes? They are doing nothing less than a work of the Church, that work by which those Japanese Christians kept a nucleus of the Church alive for two hundred years, by handing on the tradition of faith, of prayer, of a life offered to God.

Beyond this more or less hidden activity of keeping and handing on the faith inviolate, there lies a huge field for Christian witness and for taking part in works of apostleship properly so called. There are plenty of ways of testifying to Christ and exercising apostleship: they range from a quiet suggestion to a neighbour, "If I were you, I should send for a priest" or "Why not send Jim to the catechism class?", to that Christian witness that a priest also can give, but gives without the weight that a lay person's word carries. Why so? Because "that's a clergyman's job", and people know in advance that, if he speaks of God, he is bound to be "for" him. I remember a Spanish friend of mine, the general secretary of the Christian trade unions, who told me: "Part of my time I have to be giving addresses all over the country, and our chaplain comes with me to share the work. He gives the talk on social principles, and I give the talk on religion. It works best that way!"

It can be said that the "subject"—in the most exact sense of the word, that is, the responsible person—the subject of apostleship is not the bishops and priests alone but the laity too, in organic unity with them.* It is the whole parish that has responsibility for evangelizing its territory. It is the whole of the relevant

*I could again quote many authorities; see *Lay People . . .*, pp. 190–191, and cf. the quotations on p. 71.

Catholic Action organization that has responsibility for evangelizing this or that social environment. It is the whole Church, in the world for its conversion, that is the living and active sign of the Kingdom of God. And "the Church—that means *you*!", as the papal nuncio said to those gathered for the German "Catholic Day" in 1954.

Christian influence on secular affairs

When we turn to consider Christianity's influence in the life of this world we must not think only of politics in the narrow sense; we must look at the whole of public life, at social legislation, at the way technology is used, at the undertakings to spread and deepen culture, at the general atmosphere in which human beings have to live: in other words, at the whole this-wordly set-up.

The nineteenth century produced some notable lay champions of the Catholic cause, and not always without distrustful reactions from some of the clergy. One bishop, for instance, asked by what right Montalembert busied himself in the Church's concerns;* and early in the present century an intransigent French editor wrote: "It is for the Church to defend the laity, rather than for the laity to defend the Church. The Church is the strong man armed, the shepherd standing up to the wolf" (incidentally, notice this example of the word "Church" used to mean the hierarchy without the lay faithful).

These are extreme cases. What seems to me a more common nineteenth-century attitude was to count on the gentry and other big people who were influential because of their social position. Pope Pius IX himself

*Cf. *Lay People* . . ., pp. 343–344, where Newman's experience in Ireland is referred to; and see Mgr Talbot's famous remark, quoted on pp. 63–64 herein. [*Trans.*]

said it was necessary to have an effect on "il Governo".* The foundress of the Cenacle nuns, Bd Teresa Couderc, is an instructive case.† She came of farming stock, and established her society to teach school, conduct retreats for women, and other work. After a time the priest director decided that a religious congregation of that kind ought not to have a "daughter of the people" at its head, and a widowed countess was appointed in her place; Mother Couderc was allowed to sink into obscurity until her death (but at least she was not turned out of her congregation, as happened to certain other foundresses).

This happening is characteristic of an age that had not yet learnt the truth of what Lamennais, for all his extravagances, had had the merit of seeing clearly, namely: that what had formerly been done for religion by the great ones of the earth was now devolving on the people as a whole, that it was public opinion that "got things done"; and that for the future it was these new rulers who had to be turned to. Today, Catholic activity directed towards keeping or making social life Christian is no longer the responsibility of a few important people; it is a ramifying activity whose organizations are spread all over the world. What exactly is this activity in relation to the Church's mission? What is the lay people's part in it, and so, ultimately, their part in the area of the Church's mission that this action represents?

The Church has existence in herself, of her own; but she does not exist *for* herself. She has a mission, in and to the world: a mission to convert the world, and then,

*On this subject, see W. Ward's *Life of Newman*, vol. i, pp. 583–584.
†See C. C. Martindale, *Marie Thérèse Couderc* (London, 1921).

so far as may be, to keep it in the right way, directed towards God and ordered in accordance with his will.

The Church's twofold mission

"You must go out, making disciples of all nations . . .". That is the essential mission, and we have already seen that the laity share in it. For my part, I have always opposed any tendency to insist predominantly, if not exclusively, on influencing the temporal order; apostleship properly so called holds the first place, even where the laity are concerned.

But why should the Church pay attention to secular things at all? For several reasons. First, because faith and charity require it, for they cannot come to terms with just anything that turns up: some states of things are in themselves contrary to love and to faith in God, the Father of all men. Faith and love make demands which can be met in various ways, but they impose a certain minimum and absolutely refuse to condone certain situations.

There is another reason, whose cogency and importance are more and more recognized. Except in rather rare individual cases, people cannot be made Christians unless they have first been "made men". The founder of the Salvation Army wrote: "What is the use of preaching the Gospel to men whose whole attention is concentrated upon a mad, desperate struggle to keep themselves alive? . . . He will not listen to you. Nay, he cannot hear you, any more than a man whose head is under water can listen to a serman."[*] Or as St Thomas puts it, "A hungry man is to be fed, not instructed" (II–II, xxxii, 3c).

[*]General Booth, *In Darkest England* . . . (London, 1890), p. 45.

Surely that is one reason why missionaries always from the outset join to the proclaiming of the Gospel the starting of dispensaries and schools, improving the condition of women and children, teaching trades and respect for work, caring for orphans and the needy, providing leper and other hospitals. There is thus a sort of "preambles to apostleship", a little like "preambles to faith"; and as the latter are concerned with a certain healthiness of the mind, so the former are directed towards a measure of healthiness of the man and of the social environment in which he has to live and whose pressure he experiences. There is a saying that grace heals at the same time that it raises man up. It is a matter of "giving man back to himself", of restoring his dignity as a human creature made in God's image.

A world consistent with God's will, or at any rate made less contrary to it, can be offered to God, dedicated and turned towards him. This means that, God being Father of all, we must do our best to get rid of everything that fosters antagonism between men and exploitation of one by another, and try to bring about whatever encourages fellowship and service, justice and brotherhood.

A lay responsibility

By preaching the Gospel, and all that flows from it, the clergy can ensure that this action on temporal things is undertaken. To awaken and strengthen consciences in regard to what is going on in the world, big things and small, is one of the essential duties of the priesthood: for the priesthood in the messianic era has also to be prophetical. But the clergy themselves cannot *carry out* this work: except accidentally and in passing, they are not really engaged in secular life, for they are directly and exclusively committed to the service of God's kingdom. Not for them the two temporal commitments that sum up all the others: the family, through which the human race is carried on, and work in trades, professions and occupations, by means of which human welfare is provided for.

Lay people are in a very different position. As I have been trying to show for years, it seems to me that the lay state, in as much as it is proper to lay people, is not a state in which people should seek to serve God and bring about his reign by making as little as possible of their earthly commitment. On the contrary: it seems more and more clear that their state requires them to serve God in and through that commitment. They are married, they have work of one sort or another, they have political concerns, public and social duties, and it is *in and through all that* that they are called to promote God's reign in men's hearts. I believe it was from this point of view that Pope Pius XII was speaking when he addressed the newly-made cardinals on 20 February 1946. What he said on that occasion is perhaps the most profound utterance ever made about the lay state and the laity's function—which nobody else can discharge— in the Church's second mission to the world, the mission, that is, of influencing the temporal order towards God and in the ways of God. The pope said:

Before all else the Church progresses in depth, only thereafter in extent. In the first place she seeks man himself, using all her endeavours to form and fashion him, to perfect God's likeness in him. She does her work in each one's heart, but it affects the whole of life and every individual activity. In men thus formed, the Church provides a secure foundation for human society. . . .

And now, what follows for the Church? Today more than ever she must live her mission; more energetically than ever she must repulse that narrow and false conception of her spirituality and inward life which would confine her, blind and dumb, to the recesses of the sanctuary. The Church cannot shut herself up, inactive, in the privacy of her churches and thus neglect the mission entrusted to her by divine Providence, the mission to form man in his fullness and so ceaselessly to collaborate in building the solid basis of society. This mission is of her essence. Looking at her from this standpoint, it can be said that the Church is the society of those who, under the supernatural influence of grace, in the perfection of their personal dignity as sons of God and in the harmonious development of every human bent and energy, build up the mighty framework of the community of men.

From this aspect the faithful, more precisely the laity, are in the front line of the Church's life; through them, the Church is the vital principle of human society. Consequently, they particularly must have an ever more clear consciousness, not only of belonging to the Church, but of *being* the Church. . . .

"Being the Church" in the sense that the pope had already made clear, that is, in that the Church is the soul of human society and gives it a sound foundation. And it is the laity alone who can carry out this essential (though second) part of the Church's mission, because it is only they who are citizens both of the City that is above and of the earthly city, in whose temporal affairs they are engaged. Accordingly, it is they who have to fulfil the Church's mission in so far as that mission is to influence the temporal order towards God and in the ways of God. In the doing of this, the laity *are* the Church.

Past and present

I now want to put before you how, so far as I can see, the laity are *today* called to be active in the Church and for God's reign in the world. But I cannot do this without first giving a short historical sketch of the subject; not a scientific sketch but one that is, I think, correct in its broad lines (each point really needs a study to itself).

I will not dwell on the Church of antiquity, in the days of persecution and the early martyrs. From the point of view that we are concerned with, two things characterized her during that age: (1) She did not think of herself as called to bring about the christianization of secular affairs; and in any case she was not in any position to do so; (2) The priesthood did not seem to be a special "caste" in society; the distinction between clergy and laity was much less marked than it became later, and lay people took active part in the sacred duties of a Church whose attention was wholly directed towards the kingdom of Heaven.

Things changed when, in the year 313, the Church came to be at peace with the Roman empire, and especially when the emperors themselves were Christians. A sort of union or symbiosis came about between the Church and society. This was so much so that in writings of the Carolingian age the very word church, *ecclesia*, was used indifferently for both what we call The Church and what to us is temporal society: to them there was one Christian society. Of this society the emperor was the head—especially when the emperor was Charlemagne. He called himself, and councils and bishops (but not the pope) called him, head of the Church, "Caput Ecclesiae", "Rector Ecclesiae", "Rector fidelium". Society, *ecclesia*, was or was intended to be ordered according to the Church's rules and patterns and for the Church's ends: Charlemagne enacted laws to procure men's eternal salvation.*

Everything was Church. The Church governed birth and death, work and leisure, the arts and sciences, and these last were cultivated in general simply in the service of salvation and for God's glory. In fact, society was like a kind of vast monastery, whose father abbot was the emperor. In a Cistercian abbey, for example, several cultural and other activities are carried on: printing and bookbinding, a farm, a smithy and so forth, but simply to support and adorn the life of God's servants, whose sole real business is to praise him. Christendom was rather like that, in the days when Christendom meant something definite. Earthly activities, the work of this world, were almost without independence; and, being pursued solely for religious ends, there was little scope for them to develop and progress.

An uncle of the emperor Frederick Barbarossa, Otto of Freising, who was a Cistercian monk and then a bishop and a leader of a crusade, wrote in 1146 a work that he called *De duabus civitatibus*, in the course of which he used an extremely apt phrase. I have told first, he said, the story of two cities at grips with one another. But since the time of Theodosius the Great,†

---

*Fr Congar now confines himself to the Church in the West. The contemporaneous history of the Church in the Eastern empire, centred at Constantinople (Byzantium, New Rome), is very relevant to the author's theme; but it would require a quite special study. [*Trans.*]

†He became emperor at Constantinople in 379, and the Christian empire is commonly dated from this time.

"the city of this world being as it were asleep" (*tanquam sopita civitate mundi*), the whole world has been Christian; and so I have now to write the history of only one city, which I choose to call the Church. Otto was right: the earthly, temporal city was, so to speak, sleeping in the bosom of the Church.

Another characteristic of medieval Christendom was that the Church's influence on the secular world was left entirely in the hands of the secular rulers. When they were converted, they made laws in accordance with the Church's will, and the life of the society governed by these laws was *ipso facto* governed by Christianity. Before writing my *Lay People in the Church* I studied the subject as seen in tradition and the older theological writings; and my interest was aroused by the discovery that, about 1580, St Robert Bellarmine had written a work *De laicis*, Concerning the Laity. Yes; but I also discovered that it was solely concerned with kings, princes and governors. It was *them*, those lay people, on whom the Church relied to carry out her mission in relation to temporal things.

But seeds of another kind were soon striking strong roots. They did not have to wait for the "age of Enlightenment", or even for the Renaissance and the great discoveries. Were I asked to give a date for the beginning of the modern world, I should not hesitate for a moment: I should name the opening of the twelfth century. Obviously I cannot set out my reasons here, but I can recall a few facts. There was Pope Gregory VII's reform which, denouncing a confused notion of the Church which made the emperor its head, began to formulate the idea of two societies. There was the increase of trade and commerce and of populations, and then the rise of the communes, localized self-governing corporations. There were the Crusades, which fired the imagination of the West and helped on the emergence of a developed secular society. There were the more or less anti-ecclesiastical religious movements of the twelfth century.

There is abundant evidence for the growth of a certain anticlericalism; lay people protested against clergy privileges, feeling that the flock was shorn rather than fed. With the growth of a strong royal power, as in France and England, this movement took on a strength of which the measure is Pope Boniface VIII's bull *Clericis laicos* in 1296; it is well known, said this pope, that the laity have always been hostile to the clergy. Is that not a positively horrifying statement?

From crisis to crisis, from abortive reform to abortive reform on the part of the Church, from cultural advance to cultural advance, from demand for independence to demand for independence on the part of laity and sovereigns—and eventually the Protestant Reformation of the sixteenth century was reached. In one of its aspects, this was a protest of lay people, especially those of the middle class and of the nobility, against the clergy's hold over them. And this revolt was supported doctrinally by a disastrous denial of the hierarchical priesthood itself, in face of which the Church tended to increase emphasis on the dignity and prerogatives of her clergy; by so doing she ran the risk of "clericalizing" herself still more, at the very time when society was secularizing itself in reaction against this.

Politics was secularized, almost inevitably now that the West was divided religiously (Richelieu, a bishop and a cardinal, made common cause with the Protestant princes against the imperial house of Habsburg). Thought was secularized, even when the thinkers themselves were Christian believers, e.g. Descartes. From this point of view, it is the opinion of historians that the year 1680 marks the beginning of a new world, a secular, critical, rationalist world, opposed to the idea of the supernatural and to all positive revealed religion.

Nevertheless this new world took over Christian moral values, though in a secularized form: Brotherhood, Philanthropy (this word, which means something quite other than charity in its Christian sense, was coined in English about 1608; "philanthropist" is first found in 1730), and so forth. Disgusted by the quarrelling that went on between Christian churches and about Christian doctrine, philosophers sought to build human society on Reason and Nature. Soon they would be saying on Science,* that guiding-spirit of the new world that was to bring about unlimited Progress.

So a secular world came into being, *un monde laïc* as the French say, one that is independent of all church influence; a world regulated solely by Reason, Science, Technology. When, for instance, Proudhon wrote his *Justice*, he attacked a society that recognizes privileges based on a so-called sacred providential order which makes for wealth and poverty, power and helplessness; in its place he would put an order governed by Reason, which is concerned only with work and deservingness. Unhappily, all too often clergy and other Catholics opposed just claims in order to safeguard their own privileges, or simply their comfortable ways; and so these claims themselves came to have an anti-religious flavour about them, particularly in France.

*That was the starting-point of Lord Herbert of Cherbury in England; cf. C. C. J. Webb, *Studies in the History of Natural Theology* (Oxford, 1915), pp. 334 ff., and G. R. Cragg, *From Puritanism to the Age of Reason* (Cambridge 1950), pp. 74, 190 ff.

The Christian in a secularized society

I cannot go into all the stages and aspects of this process, but the result was the appearance, for the first time in history, of a wholly secular and "unsacred" world, purely of this earth and its time. I say "for the first time in history", because the ancient world of paganism was not like that, it was religious; and we have seen that during the Christian middle ages the "city of this world" was as if it slept. But the sleeping beauty has woken up, and she is now very busy. At our work and in our social life we are in constant contact, not simply with Christians who interpret Christianity in a different way from ourselves, but with professed atheists, with agnostics, with those who are puzzled, and with very many who simply do not care one way or the other. We are called to live among and with these fellows of ours, and to witness to Christ's charity before them.

The Catholic Christian may well often feel himself religiously isolated. He is like a soldier parachuted into battle: there he is, he looks about, and he cannot see a comrade nearer than seven or eight hundred yards away, out of earshot. As for the staff officers . . .? Yet it is the Christian's duty to be where he is. If he chooses to live cosily rubbing shoulders in "Catholic circles", he is then shutting himself up in a sort of ghetto. In addition to the fact that to do so would be repugnant to him as a human being, for he will want to do his bit in the world, he would in that case cease to be a witness to Christ. On the other hand, if he wants to co-operate and to witness—what an undertaking!

Let me quote a few words from Cardinal Suhard, which he wrote during the war; they set out clearly and strikingly the pastoral problem raised for the Church by the situation we are looking at: "I state this as a fact: our peoples as a whole no longer think in a Christian way; there is a gulf between them and the Christian community and, if we are to reach them, we have got to go out from amongst ourselves and go amongst them. That is the real problem. Hitherto our efforts have been almost fruitless; our ordinary Catholic Action has proved ineffectual: it is action on behalf of environments that are Catholic (at least by profession), not Catholic Action on behalf of those that are irreligious."

That is the situation, or a situation tending that way, in which Christian witness and influence has for the future to be taken to the world. We are a long way from Theodosius and Charlemagne, or even Barbarossa! There are no "princes" now; movement has to come from below, not from above, having its source in consciences, not in institutions. If the Church is to fulfil her mission to the world, it is to the laity more than ever that she has to turn: and that is what she has done. Pope Pius XI reiterated that Catholic Action, lay activity, was the answer to worldwide secularization. The laity's hour has indeed come.

In these conditions, lay people turn to their clergy— for, to the best of my knowledge, the lay advance has not once been accompanied by any undervaluation of the priesthood; on the contrary, it is characterized rather by appeals to the clergy for assistance. Lay people who want to be witnesses to Jesus Christ in a divided, secularized, non-Christian world turn to us, their clergy, asking to be strengthened with truly spiritual nutriment, I am not imagining this; I have heard them, many times, speaking to this effect:

"Your sermons no longer meet our needs. Religious books are often simply unreal. They seem to be about some sort of life midway between Heaven and earth. We are living on earth; but we want to live there really according to the Gospel: not some popularized Stoicism or Platonism, but the full Gospel and the spirit of the Beatitudes. We want to be taught a biblical, evangelical religion, nothing complicated, but something sturdy that will enable us to take on ourselves the burden of our world in a spiritual, a Christian way. 'Our world' means the world as it is, as the past has made it and as we have inherited it from that past. There is so much that we have got to take on ourselves in a Christian fashion, which implies in a spirit of responsibility, of service, of a changed heart—all the bitter fruits of capitalism and 'every man for himself', the world that has emerged from the French Revolution and scientific rationalism, from the Reformation and divisions amongst Christians, the legacy of Christians' violence and failings, as well as of Christian grace. . . . And all the present, with its bewildering problems. . . . We want the Church to help us face all that together, as a band of brothers; we ask our clergy not to give us ready-made answers, but to help us work out our own answers, with whatever difficulty, day by day; to help us to become men and women who are striving to play a Christian part in a world which has ceased to be Christian."

A pastoral need

Unquestionably all that shows the need for a new relationship between pastors and people in some respects. I do not mean, of course, in any sense that would deny or disregard the hierarchical ministry of the clergy (that, alas! is what the Reformation did), but in the sense of an organic co-operation between the two. In this connexion there has been no little talk in France of bringing about, not simply a "team" of priest and lay people, but the "clergy-laity *pair*". I like that expression. I believe it to be right. The idea of a kind of marriage between a bishop and his flock, a priest and his parish, is a traditional one, and it has found a place in canon law.

The human family is formed in God's image, it is both communal and hierarchical—as is the Holy Trinity. God is not just the God of reason, the Eternal Axiom or the Supreme Being. He is Three Persons in a perfect oneness and communion, but in such a way that there is, at the heart of this communion and equality, a hierarchy of origin: the Father is principle of all. In a similar way, the native disposition of Christianity is always that of the oneness of a brotherly fellowship within a graded order of duties and functions. Christianity does not recognize fatherhood without brotherhood: that would be paternalism—and God is Father, but he is not paternalist, he has respect for every being's freedom. It does not recognize brotherhood without fatherhood: that would be a false and anarchical equality.

This union of the two relationships is found notably in the family, which is a divine institution and also the only natural institution which is, directly and as such, taken over and made sacred by a sacrament. In the family, it is the man who wields authority. (In principle! You know well enough that he sometimes abdicates, and his sceptre goes to the woman.) But when he has to make a decision he takes account, not only of his wife, but of his children also, paying attention to their needs, their wishes, their personal reactions.

Thus daily life goes on in conditions of community and give-and-take.

It is this mutual give-and-take that I should like to see going on between priesthood and laity. The actual forms that it could take do not matter much, provided that due respect is invariably given both to fatherhood —that is, to authority—and to fellowship in community; a respect that sees in others, not simply an object,* but a subject, a person, a grown-up person. What we need is a dialogue, something that takes place between adult and responsible persons, face to face. And dialogue has two enemies: one is monologue, when only one voice speaks; the other is disorder, when everybody talks at once. "God", wrote St Paul, "is the author of peace, not of disorder" (1 Cor. 14:33).

I am convinced that along these lines there can be found more far-reaching ways of putting the Christian abilities of the laity to work, and thus the possibility of a new springtime for the Church.

*See note on p. 22.

THE LAITY AND THE CHURCH'S
PROPHETICAL OFFICE

I will group what I have to say on this matter under four successive heads, as follows:

(1) Evangelization today requires the participation of the laity.

(2) Is this doctrinally possible?

(3) Is it possible pastorally and in practice? In what forms?

(4) And under what conditions?

1. EVANGELIZATION TODAY REQUIRES THE PARTICIPATION OF THE LAITY

The Church is not something made once for all; she goes on being made continually. And the reason for this is that her essence is found, not in organizations and groupings or even in the totality of her practising members, but in men's faith. It used to be said in medieval days that the Church is not the walls but the faithful. It is a question all the time of enlisting and mustering and increasing a people for Heaven, a people amongst whom God dwells and reigns. But, on one hand, mankind is continually renewing and multiplying itself, generation after generation; and on the other, each individual person's will is changeable and needs to hear a never-ceasing call to conversion.

And so the Church is made by the word, which arouses and upholds faith, and in the first instance by the word which testifies to the fact of Christ and utters the call to conversion, what is called in Greek *kerygma*, evangelization. The saying of Martin Dibelius that "In the beginning was the Kerygma" is not true only of the literary forms and other aspects of the New Testament: it is as well a truth about the Church, an historical truth. The history of the Church and her building up is a history of the word, and, with all the authority of an inspired writing, the book of Acts of the Apostles shows us the original pattern: "By now the word of God was gaining influence, and the number of disciples in Jerusalem was greatly increasing" (Acts 6:7; cf. 8:14, 13:49, 19:20 etc.).

By saying that much I have directed attention to an unquestionable truth of very great importance (and it may be questioned whether manuals of theology about the Church give it enough attention). But I by no means claim everything for the word in the building up of the Church: I am not forgetting the sacraments, the second form of the Bread of life. Word and sacraments have in fact an organic unity: preaching is liturgical, and celebration of the mysteries ought to be prophetical, spiritually illumined by the word which conveys the meaning of the celebration to the faithful. Nevertheless, of these two forms of the Bread of life, the word comes first logically. Kerygma precedes conversion, instruction precedes baptism; and these truths have certain consequences, not only from the standpoint of pastoral care, but also from the standpoint of theology about the Church.

The missionary Church

In all this the Church is seen to be essentially missionary. The "time of the Church", that is, the time between our Lord's ascension to Heaven and his second coming, from his passover to his *parousia*, is essentially a time of mission and apostleship (cf. Acts 1:7-8); and so it is the time of that word which proclaims and converts. The fulfilment of God's saving design is what has constantly to be kept in the forefront. It is that which governs the word of the Bible, the Christian word. If we study this idea of the word in the sacred Scriptures we see that it is essentially dynamic, "all reaching out towards the future", as a German writer has put it.

Responsibility for proclaiming the word was entrusted to the twelve apostles. It is of them that it was written —notice the precision and sufficiency of the words—"He appointed twelve to be his companions, and to go out preaching at his command" (Mark 3:14). But, though it is principally theirs, God's design does not entrust this mission to the apostolic hierarchy alone—else why did Jesus join seventy-two disciples with them, and why did one hundred and twenty disciples receive the Holy Spirit along with the eleven apostles at Pentecost? (Luke 10:1; Acts 1:15).

Antecedently, in the natural order of things, we need other people if we are to make the most and best of ourselves. It is only thanks to others that we can do anything worth while, starting with our birth into this world. True enough, I get busy, and I hope not to die without having added something, however tiny, to the world's spiritual resources; but this can be done only on the foundation of what has first been given to me. Thus there is a kind of law of mediation through our fellow humans; and this is even more so in Christianity. For, the Gospel tells us, discipleship necessarily involves a spirit and works of service to others, and the better the disciple the more service; to be a disciple and to be a servant, *mathetes* and *diakonos*, are bound up together, and they diminish or increase together.*

The Gospel therefore ordains that every disciple, every follower of Christ, should in one way or another fulfil the service of transmitting the faith, of being, with and through Christ, one sent to proclaim the salvation that he brings and to bear witness to his love. This is the greatest of all services that can be rendered to others, and it is essential to the building up and growth of Christ's Church.

The need today

This has always been a universal duty, as is eloquently attested by the Fathers in the past and the popes in the present.† But it must be admitted that there is less relevant testimony to be found in the period between the Fathers and our own time. During those thirteen centuries there was first the era of medieval Christendom when, as I have shown above (pages 51–52), kings and princes were on the whole the only active lay people; and then came the age of enfeeblement, during which, with a few very remarkable exceptions, the laity had practically no active concern in the forwarding of God's kingdom: the clergy would have been the last to call on them to do so, or even to recognize that they were able to. I could give a number of examples, but the typical one is that of Mgr George Talbot, a critic of

---

*In Christ's body which is the Church each member is the servant of all: 1 Cor. 9:19–22; 2 Cor. 4:5; Gal. 5:13.

†See *Lay People* . . ., pp. 339 ff.

Newman, who wrote in 1867: "What is the province of the laity? To hunt, to shoot, to entertain. These matters they understand, but to meddle with ecclesiastical matters they have no right at all."*

It may, then, be said that history has in general seen three types of lay people: the worldly type, as known to Mgr Talbot, which is in fact the most common (No? Tell me, what do people think about, what do they talk about?); the "medieval" type, which seeks to defend the Catholic system and extend its influence, but by rather external methods, even by public pressure and "calling in the police"; and the lay person of church tradition of whom the oldest documents and the Fathers speak, the type which in its full development attains and surpasses the aims of the lay man of medieval Christendom, by other means.

There are still considerable remnants of Christendom here and there, and it is possible that in time to come there may be a new Christendom, very different from the old one; but the fact remains that at present the situation of the world is one in which Christians, and especially really believing Christians, are in a minority. And at this same moment there is also a great shortage of clergy, a tragic circumstance which in certain regions threatens to become catastrophic. But whatever the number of clergy, even supposing it were sufficient or superabundant, there would still be a disproportion, a

*E. S. Purcell, *Life of Cardinal Manning* (London, 1896), vol. ii, p. 318. Somewhat similar things were said even by Cardinal Wiseman, in *Words of Peace and Justice* (1848). Mgr Talbot accused Newman's article "On consulting the Faithful . . ." (cf. p. 37 above) of undermining the Church's foundations. Light is thrown on the incident by passages in Douglas Woodruff's introduction to Lord Acton's *Essays on Church and State* (London, 1952).

rift, between Christianity or the Church and the contemporary world. It is not only because of their fewness or unequal distribution that the clergy find themselves at a disadvantage in their efforts to reach people and deliver Jesus Christ's message to them: it is because of the nature of the change that has come over the world of twentieth-century man.

What has happened is the emergence of a profane, "not sacred", world, a world of technology; and inevitably, from the very nature of their sacred calling, the clergy are out of contact with such a world. They were quite at home in a world which, at bottom, the Church had shaped, the forms of whose existence were more or less of the same kind as those traditional in the Church; but this is no longer so. The clergy can not, or only with the greatest difficulty, be at home in a world that is wholly secular, technological, infatuated with man and his earth. On this Ascension day in the year of grace 1958, people are more interested in Sputnik III than in the Lord whom Christians worship.

It is in consequence of this state of things that the laity's hour has struck. They are called to apostleship, to the mission of proclaiming Jesus Christ, in a new way and on a far wider scale. Pius XI and Pius XII said so, repeatedly. Already, in Rome itself, there have been held two international congresses of lay apostleship, each preceded by preparatory national conferences. It is no longer conceivable that a pastoral session on Evangelization Today should omit consideration of "the laity and the Church's prophetical office".

It is a big subject, which I cannot treat in all its aspects; I will concentrate on the evangelizing work of the prophetical function.

2. BUT FIRST, IS IT DOCTRINALLY POSSIBLE FOR LAY PEOPLE TO SHARE IN THIS WORK?

You know in advance that the answer to this question is Yes. In *Lay People in the Church* I have set out at length the traditional reasons that justify this answer, and I am not going over all that again; but I want briefly to emphasize two points which directly affect practice. They are: the different kinds of "word" the Church uses in her prophetical office; and the fact that in some of them the laity too are the "subject", i.e. the person responsible, a fact grounded in the nature of the Church and the unsearchable laws of God's design for us.

i. *Forms of "the word"*

If "the word" were exclusively "dogma", doctrinal decisions to which we are bound to submit, the faithful would have only to hear and to obey. Dogma is necessary to ensure rightness of belief and that ecclesial* oneness in the faith of which St Paul writes (1 Cor. 1:10). It falls solely to the bishops, who inherit the ministry of the Apostles, to ensure this ecclesial unity, by means of a properly dogmatic rule of faith; theirs are the corresponding gifts of grace, and they alone have authority to teach and "define" doctrine. Theological development in modern times, which has taken place in a somewhat juridical atmosphere of thought and in face of the denials made by the Protestant Reformation, has given predominant consideration to this very important aspect of the matter.

*The adjective *ecclésial* has been coined in France to signify being of or pertinent to the Church, the word "ecclesiastical" (in French as in English) having acquired an almost purely clerical connotation. Cf. *Lay People . . .*, pp. 50–51. [*Trans.*]

66

However, "defining" is but a second duty (though not secondary!) of the prophetical office, one that is wholly relative to what is needed for the proper conservation of the sacred testimony. The first duty is to "keep the word"—that lovely expression, which the Challoner-Douay translation of the Bible uses of our Lady, herself a type of the Church: "Mary kept all these words, pondering them in her heart" (Luke 2:19, 51). Faithful keeping of the word and bearing witness are the fundamental duty, and other things follow from it, even before the "defining" function; namely, the acts of teaching (*didakhe*) and of pastoral exhortation (*parenesis* or *paraklesis*), which recent writers distinguish one from the other.

ii. *The laity also have a responsibility*

Now the lay faithful, collectively and each one personally to the extent that he is a living member of the whole, are also responsible for this conservation and this witnessing.* At baptism, the faith is committed to them, as a "deposit" sealed by the Holy Spirit; they become responsible for it when they are given grace and power to be *fideles*, faithful. In former times this was expressed ceremonially in the course of preparation for baptism, by the *traditio symboli*, when they were given the baptismal summary of the faith, and the *redditio symboli*, when each made personal profession of that faith. Baptism finds its completion in confirmation. One of the essential effects of confirmation is that it makes the baptized person a witness to Jesus Christ in the world of men. He ceases to be a child in Christ, living, as little children do, for himself alone; he becomes a *man* in Christ, with his own place in the world of

*See *Lay People* . . ., pp. 259–272.

men and with the mission and the grace to bear witness to his Lord in it, by the profession, or better, the confession of the faith. We shall see later what forms this profession or confession can take.

I am in full agreement with Father Karl Rahner* that, in settling the condition proper to the laity, the decisive factor is that their Christian function is determined *by their situation in the world* : that is, by their natural commitment to the work of the world, which they do not give up in order to serve God's kingdom. They have to give glory to God, *not* by withholding themselves from that work, but precisely *in it*, and *through it*.

But it must not be forgotten—and perhaps Father Rahner has not gone into this sufficiently—that the lay person, without leaving the lay state, is characterized as Christian by the mission and grace conferred at baptism and confirmation, as a member, that is, of the ecclesial community which is called to keep the word and confess it before men. Accordingly, the lay person not only receives a Christian mission in temporal things, but also a mission in the Church as the ark and sign of faith: in the Church as ark, that he may help truly to keep the faith; as sign, that he may profess and confess the faith in the world and before men's eyes.

For they are the Church too

We must always be careful rightly to understand in what sense the word "Church" is being used. Very often it is used to mean simply the Church's government, the

*See K. Rahner, "L'apostolat des laïcs", in *Nouvelle Revue théologique*, January 1956, pp. 3–32. I had already been taking this line since 1950, but less effectively than he does; cf. *Lay People* . . ., ch. i.

bishops, what St Augustine calls the *praesules Ecclesiae*, the leaders or directors of the Church; and when that is done the Church is being looked at only as an organ of mediation between Christ and mankind. I could give dozens, hundreds, of examples of this. One is enough, and it comes from the German national catechism of 1925.*

Q. Why did Jesus found his Church?
A. Jesus founded his Church so that she might lead all men to everlasting bliss.
Q. What does the Church have to do for men?
A. The Church has to teach men, to make them holy and to lead them.

It is plain that the word Church here signifies only hierarchical mediation, and that the laity do not form this "Church"; they simply represent the "men" on whom "the Church" acts so as to teach, sanctify and direct them: in one word, they are *an object*† of priestly hierarchical activity.

This is not good theology. In sound ecclesiology,‡ the laity also *are* the Church. Time and again lately bishops have pointed out in their pastoral letters that the Church is *all* the faithful united in Christ. Pope Pius XII repeated it several times, notably in his address on 20 February 1946: "The faithful, more precisely the laity, are in the front line of the Church's life. . . .

---

*This catechism was replaced in Germany in 1955, by a new one, which has been translated into English, *A Catholic Catechism* (London, 1957); its paras. 1, 2, 48–53 show the advance made on that of 1925.

†See note on page 22.

‡I.e., theology concerning the Church. The S.O.E.D. (2nd edn., 1939) gives only an architectural meaning to this word. [*Trans.*]

Consequently, they particularly must have an ever more clear consciousness, not only of belonging to the Church, but of *being* the Church, that is, the community of the faithful on earth, under the guidance of the common head, the Pope, and of the bishops in communion with him."*

The Church is an organic body. On the one hand, each member, each cell of this body is living; on the other, all the members do not have the same function in the body, and so its one single soul, the Spirit of Christ, does not animate all the members for the same purpose and in the same way. Some, the faithful laity (and the members of the hierarchy in as much as they are in the first place among the faithful) are given spiritual vitality that they may cherish, profess and bear witness to the faith. Others, the hierarchy as such, are vitalized that they may guarantee and define the faith, and teach it with authority. But all, complete with their differences, form one single "subject", one single responsible person, and that is the *Ecclesia*, the Church.† So therefore all organically form a single subject that is responsible where witness and evangelization are concerned, proper allowance being made for the differences between the hierarchical mandate, with its pertinent powers and graces, and the simple responsibility that is common to all the faithful.

Such is the doctrine that has been propounded to us for several decades by many theologians, pastors and bishops, and by the pope himself. I will quote only the words, first, of the collective pastoral letter of the Dutch bishops in 1954, and then those of Cardinal Suhard in

*Other quotations in *Lay People . . .*, p. 49.
†See *Lay People . . .*, pp. 276 ff.; and cf. C. Journet, *The Church of the Word Incarnate* (London, 1955), vol. ii.

his pastoral *Le Prêtre dans la Cité* of 1949, which are specially relevant to what I am saying.*

Our clergy must appreciate yet more that the laity are not simply the object of the pastoral ministry, but that they have also to take part actively in the liturgy, and in apostleship and Catholic Action as they have been doing effectively for some time in the social field; they are adult members of Holy Church, and they wish to have their say in the building up of the mystical Body, of which they seek to be conscious members.

So the priest's apostolic task is clear. Face to face with men who have got to be saved, he will not say "I", but "we". It is not simply the lay person, nor is it the priest by himself, who is the master workman of evangelism—it is the Christian community. The basic cell, the unit of measurement, in apostleship is everywhere a sort of organic compound, and inseparable two-in-one of clergy-laity.

Grounded in God

All this is grounded in the nature of the Church as an organic body, and in God's "plan" for us; more still, like all things ultimately (for all things have something Godlike in them), it is grounded in what I would be so daring as to call God's very structure. We see that from beginning to end his pattern combines a principle of community with a principle of hierarchy, of ordered ranks. I have shown this is true of the Church by reference to her priestly, kingly, prophetical and

*For other passages, see *Lay People* . . ., pp. 357–358.

apostolic functions. It could be shown to be true also of human society, from the family community up to the political nation, with all the intermediate groupings, professional, economic and the rest. Two principles, of hierarchy and of brotherhood, have to work together in harmony. Neither one may be upheld without the other: hierarchy without brotherhood is paternalism; brotherhood without hierarchy is bogus democracy and anarchy. It is rather like what Pascal said of the Church: "A multitude that does not form a unity is a jumble; a unity that does not depend on the multitude is tyranny."

In the end it all goes back to the fact that God himself is at the same time both unity and plurality: absolutely one in nature and perfection, in life and glory, more than one in the three Persons who share fully and completely this nature and perfectness. God himself is hierarchy and fellowship: hierarchy, because the Son and the Spirit proceed from the Father, who is the Principle-without-principle, *Fons Deitatis*, the well-spring of Godhead; fellowship, because the Father, the Son and the Holy Spirit are one and never energize apart from one another. There is as it were a kind of concelebration* between them; and in every aspect of her life, in apostleship or in faith as in liturgical worship, the Church on earth has to strive to reproduce the transcendent example.†

---

*The celebration of the Mysteries by two or more celebrants together, all consecrating the same bread and wine, as at the ordination of priests and bishops and more frequently in some Eastern liturgies. [*Trans.*]

†For the basis in the mystery of the Holy Trinity of the laws governing relations between hierarchy and people, see *Lay People . . .*, pp. 271, 280–281.

3. IS IT PASTORALLY AND PRACTICALLY POSSIBLE FOR LAY PEOPLE TO SHARE IN THIS WORK? HOW?

I have already foreshadowed an affirmative answer to this question by showing that "the word" takes a variety of forms. It is very common teaching among the Fathers of the Church that, before the ministry of the sacraments and jointly with it, the imparting of the faith is the principal activity by which the Church exercises her motherhood. Time and again the Fathers tell us that by believing we bring Christ to birth in ourselves, and that we bring him to birth in others by propounding the faith to them and helping them to accept it. They, the Fathers, constantly relate the Church's motherhood to that of Mary who, says St Augustine, conceived wholly and only because of her faith in the angel's message.* Thus the motherhood of Mary and the motherhood of the Church are essentially virginal; in either case Christ is begotten virginally through faith: it is one and the same mystery that is brought about, first perfectly in the type, the Virgin Mary, and then in the Church. It is for this reason that Father Hugo Rahner has so aptly called the Church "the Mary of world-history".

Obviously the Church's motherhood is principally exercised through the priestly clergy, especially when— again following the Fathers—we consider the part played in it by the sacraments, jointly with faith. But it is certainly not in accordance with the perfect balance of patristic theology (notably St Augustine's) in this matter to say with M. J. Scheeben: "Strictly speaking,

*See J. C. Plumpe, *Mater Ecclesia: an Inquiry into the Concept of the Church as Mother in Early Christianity* (Washington, 1943); and H. Rahner, *Marie et l'Église* (Paris 1955), passim, especially chs. iii and vi.

the Church's motherhood does not belong to the totality of her members, but only to those entrusted with her fertilizing and priestly powers which raise up, nurture and rule the children of God."* The answer is again to recall that the Church's motherhood is, like the word, manifested in various ways. There is the keeping of the faith and there is its definition, there is teaching with public authority and there is teaching privately, and so on.

I cannot go into all the considerations here, even in respect of those activities that are proper to lay people within the sphere of the Church's prophetical office. For example, I must leave aside, in spite of its great importance, the laity's part in the increase of religious knowledge, in theology, in vindication of the faith, too, and in its showing forth through the different activities of a Christian culture. I must here ignore mystical knowledge. I cannot go into the laity's contribution to the development of Catholic teaching (for instance, in matters of anthropology or of social doctrine—a field in which they are normally particularly active), or to properly dogmatic development, a matter that has recently come to the fore again with reference to teaching about our Lady.† All that would take us much too far. I will stick to my term of reference: Evangelization today; what is the laity's part in it?

The laity's part in practice

I referred just now to the *traditio* and *redditio symboli* in that preparation and instruction for baptism which is called "catechesis". In Christianity's early days, when

Die Mysterien des Christentums, §80; French trans., *Le Mystère de l'Église* (1946), p. 97.
†See *Lay People* . . ., pp. 258 ff., the whole chapter.

it was mostly adults who were baptized, this catechesis naturally came before baptism; it was an act of the Church, through her priests, in response to a personal movement of approach to the faith. Today, of course, baptism of the newly-born is by far the more common; and when the parents present a baby to be baptized it is a promise on their part that the child shall undergo the Church's catechesis after baptism, that is, that they will in due course "send him to catechism": but it is also a promise themselves to give him a Christian upbringing.

We clergy know only too well what a world of difference there is between the children of a Christian family, wherein our teaching of them is backed by all the home influence, and the children of indifferent or hostile parents, from whom we get no help or support at all. When the *traditio* and *redditio symboli* come *after* the sacramental act of baptism (that is, nearly always in ordinary circumstances), the parents then share in our work of *traditio symboli*, "instruction", to the extent of at least half. Remember how, under the Old Covenant of God's people, Jewish parents ensured the handing on of faith in the living God (in "Jahveh who brought us out of the land of Egypt") and knowledge of his mighty works; it was the duty of the father of a family to explain the meaning of the Passover to his children (Exod. 12:25–27). It is the duty of Christian parents to ensure the tradition, the faithful handing on from generation to generation, of the faith, of the love for God, of prayer, of Christian moral behaviour.

Thus parents are, highly effectively and without any show, sharers in the work of tradition or transmission in the most theological sense of the word. I am in full agreement with Father W. Wilmers, who wrote in 1851:

"This real propagation [of the faith] is not wholly identified with the ecclesiastical magisterium. This magisterium, or rather the exercise of it, represents *one mode* of propagation. But all the faithful, especially parents when they teach the faith to their children, have part in propagating or handing on the deposit of faith."*

Do not imagine that parents are doing a small thing when they proclaim the Gospel as the Church has to do. Did not St Augustine tell fathers of families that they are a kind of bishop?† But let us now turn our attention to the laity, no longer in their families, the cells of the Church, but in the public ecclesial community, that is, concretely, as members of a parish and of other religious groupings and undertakings, such as Catholic Action.

I have shown that lay people share in the trust committed to the Church to proclaim Jesus Christ. But, unlike the hierarchical mandate given to priests, which is precise and personal, the laity's mission is somewhat indefinite and its incidence collective. There are exceptions, of course, for a lay person can be given a clear mission, formally by mandate or arising out of circumstances. For instance suppose a man who alone is in a position to rescue his neighbour who is in jeopardy: the circumstances show God's will for him, he is faced with a responsibility, and so has a clear mission.

The laity and the Church as sign

A first form of the laity's participation in the Church's evangelizing function is their more or less active part in

*Lehrbuch der Religion, vol. i, §13 (3rd edn., Munster, 1894); the editor of the 8th edn. (1922) deleted the quoted passage. Cf. *Lay People . . .*, pp. 282–283.

†He was quoted by Pope Pius XII in his encyclical letter *Summi pontificatus*. Cf. *Lay People . . .*, p. 193.

the Church's duty of being a sign of God's kingdom before the eyes of the world. This duty falls on the Church as a whole, but it also falls on each local community, and it is at that level that I want to consider it.

The obligation in question is concerned with the general method of proclaiming the Gospel and drawing people to the faith, which is a method of signs and symbols (see St John's gospel). Jesus offered men signs, generally parables and miracles, but also himself in his own person. Under those signs the kingdom of Heaven was brought close, and opportunity was given to recognize and accept that approach—or to refuse it: for example the parable of the great supper (Luke 14:15–24) and the miracle of the man born blind (John 9); and there was the sign that Jesus himself is, for "nobody has ever spoken as this man speaks" (*ib.*, 7:46). According to the way a man reacts to the sign he has encountered, so an attitude begins to take shape within him; either one of good will and welcome which, God helping, will lead to faith, or one of ill will and refusal, which will lead to a stubborn turning-away from God's invitations—such a one "will be unbelieving still, though one should rise from the dead" (Luke 16:31). Whilst Christ was on earth it was in this way, by encountering a sign, that men were enabled to see that the kingdom of God was at hand.

Now that Jesus is no longer amongst us in human form, it is through the Church that the sign comes to men, and this in very many ways. Exceptionally, there are still miracles; there is the occurrence of holiness great beyond the ordinary; there is preaching that is infused with unusual gifts. Sometimes, the heavens open and the Gospel becomes clear and compelling, as clear, compelling, and alive as when Jesus Christ still walked the earth. But, short of these less common signs, there is also the daily life of the Church, with all her aspects that are open to men's sight, things which are signs to mankind that God's kingdom has drawn near to us, that it is open, awaiting us. I am thinking, for one example, of all those expressions of Christianity in the realm of art and culture—such a thing as that standing sign the cathedral of Chartres, which goes on offering to so many pilgrims the Christian message that can be read in its beauty and its modesty. I am thinking, for another example, of those shining lights of Christian life in common, religious communities; a monastery or convent is a sign, it is a revelation of the kingdom of God, a call to faith and to God's service. Mark the telling words that are carved on the choir-screen at the abbey of Maria-Laach: "I, a prisoner in the Lord, beseech you that you walk worthy of the vocation in which you are called" (Eph. 4:1).

But I am also thinking of communities of lay people. That society of homes, a parish whose people love one another—there too is a sign of God's grace, a call to Christian living. (A parish often reflects the atmosphere of its presbytery, and the first element of the sign is the brotherliness between the clergy.) Or again, a single Christian home is a sign, with its equal balance of freedom and deference; a good home is a striking thing. All these enter into the great sign which the Church is. Think, too, how a warm-hearted friendliness, a token of true sympathy, a kindly neighbourliness, testifies to the charity of Christ.* And finally, think of the sign

---

*Two examples from history. (1) The part played in St Augustine's conversion by the welcome given him by St Ambrose at Milan (cf. J. J. O'Meara, *The Young Augustine*, London, 1954); (2) St Pachomius (d. 348) while still a heathen

provided by a properly communal celebration of the Eucharist, by a parish at worship. I still feel the impression of supreme conviction in testifying to the faith that I experienced when taking part in the Holy Week and Easter offices in certain Alsatian parishes. When they celebrate thus, united with their priests, united by their priests in a single *Ecclesia*, the faithful are indeed *bearing witness to the Mysteries*. The liturgy has an incomparable value for evangelization, provided that the sign is genuine and recognizable.

Furthermore, a lay man may be called on to proclaim God's word during the liturgy by reading the epistle and gospel in the people's tongue (and this whether dressed in cassock and surplice and standing near the sanctuary, or simply getting up in his place among the congregation). Their baptismal consecration makes lay people "liturgical persons", members of God's People as distinct from not-consecrated men, who are not of God's People (cf. 1 Peter 2:10).

In this matter of the sign that is shown by the whole Church, and by the laity in particular, in the celebration of God's praises, a place must be given to singing and to hymns, a modest place but an important one. Everywhere and in every age men need to make use of poetical forms to arrive at and express spiritual things, and it is the great ages of Christian religious renewal that have best met this demand for beauty of form. Christian men need a Christian poetry, and missionaries require poetic means whereby to convey truth. Music and song

---

was conscripted into the army, and as a recruit received kindness from the inhabitants of a Christian village in Egypt. He was much impressed, and this was the beginning of the conversion of the man who became the father of communal monasticism.

are one of the greatest attractions of our day; in *La nouvelle vague* (Paris, 1958), F. Giroud has commented on the number of people who, to the question "What would you most dislike to be deprived of?", answered "Gramophone records." Singing is a channel that can convey many elements of religion, it can bear testimony and be in its way a real proclamation of the good news of Jesus Christ.* Rejoice!—we have St Paul behind us (cf. Eph. 5:19–20; Col. 3:16).

Let me insist on an important point. When referring to baptism of the newly-born, I said that this involved the necessity of a catechesis after baptism. But we must go further than that. When an adult receives faith and comes to be baptized, he has made a weighty choice and undergone a true conversion. Now, one of the formidable consequences of the practice of infant baptism is that the moment of personal conversion is passed over, whether as regards the life of the baptized themselves or as regards the activities, or even the pastoral pre-occupations and ideas, of the Church.

There is an extremely serious danger here. The success of religious sects† is partly explained by the fact that they call for personal conversion, whereas this call is scarcely heard in the corresponding activities of the Church. The sects make much of "revivalism", that is, they appeal for conversion and little else; the Church imparts her catechesis, that is, instruction, without appealing for conversion. The two things ought to be

*Cf. Eric Gill, *Autobiography* (London, 1940), pp. 186–187: "There, at Louvain, after the slow procession of incoming monks and the following short silence when I first, all unprepared and innocent, heard *Deus, in adjutorium* . . ., I knew, infallibly, that God existed and was a living God. . . ." [*Trans.*]

†In France this is something new, following the last war.

joined. I make my own the words of a German writer, H. Greeven, in a recent study of the *Aemter*, ministries, in the writings of St Paul: "Prophecy without Doctrine degenerates into fanaticism; Doctrine without Prophecy becomes frozen with legalism."

Is this all going too far? Surely it is not putting too heavy a responsibility on Christians to say that they have a duty, in their personal lives, their activities and their communities, to show forth the signs or parables of the kingdom of God which are so many calls to conversion, conversion not only of unbelievers but also of themselves and of other Christians. It is indeed incumbent on every Christian to do his part with his fellows to enable the Church to be an evangelizing power in the world. Evangelization means putting before men the fact of Jesus Christ, of his call to them, of his deeds that set them free. To evangelize—you know well enough—is not simply to preach dogmatic truth and obtain the adhesion of someone, who thereafter will turn up at Mass; it is to bring Jesus Christ and his sovereign claims into men's lives, into their real, ordinary, daily lives as well as into those occasions when they are faced by hard and important choices.

I have sketched out a scheme of things that may seem to you a bit unreal. What does it actually involve? It involves taking the moral and spiritual demands of the Christian Gospel very seriously, going well beyond meritorious "practices", which can be used to satisfy systematic Catholic requirements without really answering the calls of the Gospel. It involves taking prayer seriously, and the Cross, and brotherly love in a spirit of humbleness and service; it involves getting at the truth of what we say and do in church, and avoiding mere ritualism, which can be a threat not only to public worship but to preaching, "good works", and other things as well. . . .

The word completes the sign

Word and sign go together in the Gospel. The sign has its full value only when it is illumined by the word. So we must now turn to the word itself, and here too lay people have their part. There are several ways of teaching. A backward child may be brought home and taught the elements of religion in the simplest form. A lay person can teach catechism officially, by agreement with the parish priest, or because he has been officially commissioned to do so, a true *missio canonica*. A lay person can study sacred subjects and teach them as scientific disciplines; he can be invited by episcopal authority to be a member of committees that study and work out the implications of doctrine or of pastoral care. Most especially, bishops look for the lay contribution in social matters and in problems set by new techniques, when it is a question of judging and guiding them in the light of the Gospel.*

Confession of faith can be made through one's private life or by personal activity; it is safe enough to confess Christ in London or New York, in Paris or Bonn, but it is quite another matter in East Berlin or in Shanghai. . . . It can take an organized form, dedicated by an official mandate, in Catholic Action properly so called; in that case, lay people receive a part in the hierarchy's own

*Cf. *Lay People* . . ., pp. 254–255, 273–274, 297. "In social questions, the laity must apply the principles that the Church lays down; but they also have a teaching function in certain fields that require technical knowledge and practical experience" (Mgr Richaud, Archbishop of Bordeaux, in an address to employers, 1953).

responsibility, at any rate if Pope Pius XI's definition of Catholic Action is strictly adhered to.

It is clear that the testimony to and teaching of the faith given in these ways by lay people can in some respects be more apostolically effective than that given by clergy. To speak of God is our job as priests, and people know in advance that when we speak of him we shall be "on his side". In his Memoirs, Leo Trotsky relates how when he was a boy at Odessa he went to a school where many of the pupils were German Protestants, and at the beginning of term all were assembled for a sermon. Young Trotsky was much impressed by the solemn atmosphere of the discourse; but he did not understand German, and he asked his neighbour what the preacher had actually said. The boy replied, "He said what it was proper to say."

Yes, it is like that. We clergy, unless we have a bit of the prophet in us, say what we are obliged to say. But when lay people speak of God, it is taken for granted that they are doing so because they believe in him, and not because it is their job to do so. There can be a more prophetical quality in their words. Furthermore, being actively concerned in the world's affairs, they are more sensitive than the clergy to its "vibrations." The expressions of the faith that they propound on the cultural plane or relating to human commitments inspired by the faith, are sometimes less well balanced than those of the clergy, but they often have more life and "guts", and a better "tone" too. It is not easy to imagine a Bernanos in a cassock; and few of his writings would have survived the ordeal of scrutiny for a *nihil obstat.*

The value of asking questions

This is a convenient place to refer to a way, if not of teaching directly, of co-operating in the Church's teaching activity, which is open to lay people and which in fact they do, thank God, make use of. I mean, asking questions of their priests and bishops, and making known their wishes (not demands).

Long experience of teaching and of intellectual life has convinced me that it is questions above all that bear fruit, they are the living seed. The worth of an answer is the worth of the question that has evoked it. Answers without questions answer nothing, literally: they may be customary ritual words, but they are not the living word—all the life has gone out of it. I respectfully invite my brothers in the ministry to join me in an examination of conscience. We have a means of making our work more fruitful, and our answers too if we are able to reach that far—by being open to questions from anybody, and therefore from the laity. Let me tell you something that I have learned, not by deduction from a general principle but by induction from observed facts. I looked about me and I saw a number of different priests or groups of clergy who were outstandingly effective, and I asked myself what accounted for the special quality of all that they said. The answer was plain: all were priests who lived in close contact with lay people, "in dialogue" with them, always welcoming their questions.

Not that the laity stop short at asking questions to which they await an answer that is like Athene springing fully armed from the brain of Zeus, "The Church says . . ." (once again, what exactly does "Church" mean here?). No. When they formulate their problems or their desires they also make suggestions. Answers and standpoints are worked out *together*, with proper give-and-take. So here the clergy have a way of learning* (and correlatively, the laity a way of teaching), which appears to me to be very effective wherever it is whole-heartedly carried out. It is noticeable that problems, requests and suggestions from the laity come with an accent of truth; they are plumb on the spot, genuine. It follows that they are also exacting. It is very different from "what it is proper to say".

I believe that clergy who have experimented along these lines will subscribe to the words of a Provençal priest, a Workers' Catholic Action chaplain: "When I was without laity for three years I had the feeling of an empty priesthood." It was St John Chrysostom, himself a bishop, who called the laity "the bishop's priestly *pleroma*, plenitude". I believe that these statements, like my well-loved expression "clergy-laity pair", present in figurative form something that is very strictly true.

4. CONDITIONS FOR DOING THIS WORK

The first condition is of course a fervent life of the spirit. And, since I am a cleric, you will expect me to say "what it is proper for a cleric to say", to wit, that one must be religious, one must pray, and so on. I may surprise you, but I *do* say that, and, what is more, I *believe* it! But I say it and I believe it at a different level from that of edifying moral phrases. I believe it

---

*As St Cyprian says: "It behoves bishops not only to teach but also to learn" (*Ep.* lxxiv, x, i); cf. St Augustine, quoting 2 Tim. 2:24, and Cyprian's own example, *De baptismo*, iv, 5, 7; v, 26, 37 (P.L., vol. 43, cc 158, 194).

because I believe in the mystery of apostleship, because I believe apostleship is a mystery, giving that word its fullest meaning and all its weight.

Evangelization, the proclamation of the Good News, means nothing less than putting into effect the *sequentia sancti Evangelii*, "the continuation of the holy Gospel". Open your Bible and turn to the most concrete of the four written gospels, St Mark's; it starts off, "The beginning of the good news (gospel) of Jesus Christ, the Son of God", and goes on to tell of the preaching of John, the baptizer and forerunner. But the most profound of the gospels, St John's, takes that beginning back to before the earthly history of salvation, back to the bosom of the Father, to whom is ascribed *agape*, the love that gives and from which proceeds the Word. Whether we be clergy or laity, our proclamation, our showing forth of the Gospel means nothing less than to carry forward, to the end of time and the limits of space, that saving Word which was born eternally from the bosom of the Father and began to be heard in time nearly two thousand years ago in Palestine. "The Holy Spirit will come upon you, and you will receive strength from him; you are to be my witnesses in Jerusalem and throughout Judaea, in Samaria, yes, and to the ends of the earth"*: those words are our commission to carry this work on.

As you see, this is quite a different thing from "Doing propaganda", and quite a different thing from being successful on this earth. The propagandist, the publicity man, is simply doing a job, for which he works out a technique. The apostle lives the mystery of the manifestation of God, lives it in his own poor bodily life: "We have this treasure in earthen vessels" (2 Cor. 4:7).

*Acts 1:8. Cf. Matt. 28:19–20; Mark 16:15; Luke 24:47–49.

He has to be sanctified before being sent out into the world, cleansed and made holy by the word received in faith, as Jesus sets forth in the gospel according to St John.* It is not only a matter of being very religious and good; it is more than that. It means becoming a whole human creature for Christ's sake,† a human being captured, occupied, possessed, vitalized by faith. Again, when I say "faith" I mean another thing and more than a simple profession of the truths in the Catechism (though of course this is included). I mean biblical faith in the living God, boundless open-hearted trust, constantly renewed, that he will rule my life, live his mystery in me and radiate his love through me.

It all comes to this, that evangelization is to show forth God, to enable his light to be seen everywhere. I even venture to put it this way, that evangelization is to live and work in order that God may be God and be recognized as God, not only in himself—he is that, with or without us, and we cannot add or subtract an iota—but in the world. This is what was meant by a second-century Jewish rabbi, Simeon ben Yohai, when he said, "If you are witnesses to me, then I am God!" (cf. Isaias, 43:12). I will end on that profound saying, commending it to your faithful observance.

*Cf. Fr Congar's *Mystery of the Church* (London 1960), pp. 44–45. Read especially John 17:14 ff.

†Cf. Dorothy Dohen, *Vocation to Love* (New York, 1950; London 1959), ch. ii: "If the lay apostle has the vocation to restore all things in Christ, then it follows that he has the vocation *to be Christ*, or, in other words, to be a *humanity* for Christ—a humanity for Christ in whom the Word can again be made flesh, to fulfill his mission of establishing order and harmony between God and man, of saving souls, and founding a society that will be conducive to the saving of souls" (pp. 26–27), and this whatever a person's state of life: Christ can be shown forth by a school-master, a navvy, a housewife, from an invalid's bed, in every human condition.